JUST A MINUTE MORE

Just a Minute More

Glimpses of Our Great Canadian Heritage

Marsha Boulton

McArthur & Company

Toronto

Canadian Cataloguing in Publication Data

Boulton, Marsha
    Just a minute more: glimpses of our great
Canadian heritage

ISBN 1-55278-072-4

1. Canada – History – Miscellanea.   2. Questions
and answers. I. Title.

FC176.B67 1999   971'.002   C99-930005-9
F1026.6.B68 1999

Composition and Design by Michael P. Callaghan
Typeset at Moons of Jupiter, Inc. (Toronto)
Cover Design by Rocco Baviera/4 Eyes Art + Design
Printed in Canada by Best Book Manufacturers

McArthur & Company
322 King Street West, Suite 402
Toronto, ON, M5V 1J2

10 9 8 7 6 5 4 3 2 1

Printed in Canada

TABLE OF CONTENTS

Acknowledgements / ix

✧

PART TWO

Innovation & Invention 63

PART FOUR

HEROES, HEROINES & THE ODD SCOUNDREL . . 169

Acknowledgements

My father was a secret agent in the Second World War. However, I grew up thinking that he had been a member of the Canadian Army Dental Corps.

Dad kept his military vow of secrecy for fifty years, until one fateful Christmas when he gave each member of the Boulton family a neatly bound memoir of his derring-do service years.

History makes a great gift, especially when it is so unexpected.

In this book, my third volume of ancedotal glimpses of our Canadian heritage, I hope the reader will find many unexpected aspects of our collective past.

Archivists, scholars and librarians across Canada have assisted me in the discovery process. Sometimes they even provoked me. I do not think Will James aficionado Allan Jensen would have allowed me to leave the Medicine Hat Museum and Art Gallery without making sure I had a folio of information about his hero.

Sincere thanks are extended to all of those who provided vital information, as well as infectious enthusiasm. My companion, author Stephen Williams, has served as both a critical eye and a mentor with a sense of humour. He knows, all too well, the line a writer walks when truth is stranger than fiction. I also wish to thank my publisher Kim McArthur and the sterling team at McArthur & Company for their support and sagacity. It is my privilege to be a part of their bold new Canadian publishing enterprise.

ORIGINALS
&
UPSTARTS

THE MILLENNIAL TREE

TO WALK WITH GIANTS

NO PRISON IN THE WOODS

THE COLOUR OF THE OLD WEST

SIR BARTON AND THE COMMANDER

THESE BOOTS WERE MADE FOR WALKIN'

LADYLIKE AND LETHAL

LILY OF THE MOHAWKS,
GENEVIÈVE OF NEW FRANCE.

THE MILLENNIAL TREE

Pacific Coast, 1824 — It is the largest tree in Canada, achieving heights of twenty storeys. More than 1,000 growth rings have been counted on stumps as wide as an average single-lane roadway, making it a truly millennial tree.

The Douglas fir (*Pseudotsuga taxifolia*) is a majestic, blue-crowned tree. Its wood became the core of British Columbia's forest products industry. The botanist whose name it is taken from first discovered the tree at Mt. St. Helens in Washington State on one of his many expeditions to discover new species.

Today, groves of Douglas fir mark David Douglas's 1799 birthplace in Scone, Scotland and the site of his mysterious death in 1834 on the Big Island of Hawaii. But the Douglas fir is not his only legacy, since in his short lifetime David Douglas contributed approximately 7,000 previously unknown species of plants to our understanding of the natural world. He has been called a "Botanical Columbus."

The son of a Perthshire stonemason, Douglas was attracted to nature from an early age. By the age of eleven he was serving as an apprentice gardener on large estates where access to botanical libraries stimulated his interest in exotic plants. Further study took him to the Glasgow Royal Botanic Garden and at the age of twenty-four, Douglas became a field collector for the Horticultural Society of London.

In 1823, the Society sent him on a four-month expedition that began in New York and saw the intrepid Scot travelling as far as Amherstburg in Upper Canada and Sandwich (now Windsor, Ontario). Despite the fact that he was robbed of his money and his coat while climbing a tree, Douglas managed to return to Britain with an impressive array of samples.

The following year, he was sent to explore the Pacific coast of North America. Fort Vancouver, a Hudson Bay Company outpost on the Columbia River, served as his headquarters. One of the many samples he sent back to London in his first shipment was his namesake evergreen, whose wood Douglas suggested "may be found very useful for a variety of domestic purposes."

Indeed the multi-faceted Douglas fir had not gone unnoticed before Douglas. Native people used the flat-needled boughs as covering on the floors of their lodges and as fuel for their cooking pits. The sturdy wood was useful for making everything from fish hooks to handles.

In 1778, Captain James Cook cut spars for one of his ships from the abundant forest near present-day Duncan, B.C. Exceptionally durable, Douglas fir has been used in heavy construction such as wharves, trestles and bridge parts. When thin layers are bonded together the result is a tough plywood.

In 1827, Douglas accompanied the Hudson Bay Company's annual express to York Factory on the shores of Hudson's Bay. While he got along well with fur traders and native people, Douglas had little use for the HBC, which he considered a soulless "mercenary corporation." When travelling by canoe he said that he felt "molested out of my life by men singing their boat songs." Fortunately, much of his work was a solitary endeavour.

"Being well rested by one o'clock I set out with a view of ascending what seemed to be the highest peak on the north," he wrote during his travels through the Athabasca Pass.

That day the rugged Scot climbed a rugged mountain in five hours alone and without benefit of climbing equipment. It was the earliest recorded climb in the Canadian Rockies. Douglas named his conquest Mount Brown in honour of botanist Robert Brown, the first head of the British Museum's botanical department.

He returned to England in 1827, having survived a violent storm in Hudson Bay that nearly took his life. The plants and seeds he brought with him were the largest collection ever gathered by one person.

Although he was notably shy, Douglas became an instant celebrity.

Three years later, he returned to Fort Vancouver and continued to botanize despite diminishing eyesight caused by the blowing snow, sand and glaring sun experienced during his previous adventures. Still, one of his travelling companions noted that he would "scramble like . . . a cat upon rocks" when a specimen attracted his attention. A few years later, he lost sight completely in his right eye, but was determined to return to England, travelling through British Columbia, to Alaska and then across Siberia.

His ambitious journey was foiled in a misadventure on the Fraser River when he lost his canoe over a cataract near Prince George, B.C. Douglas and his guide were caught in a whirlpool and washed up on the rocks. While he was lucky to be alive, more than 400 specimens and his meticulous notes were lost. Five days after the incident, Douglas was bound for the Sandwich Islands, reaching Honolulu just before Christmas, 1834.

What happened next remains something of a mystery. Douglas apparently continued to collect specimens with his usual vigour in Hawaii. In July, he was exploring on the slope of Mauna Kea in northern Hawaii. His body was ultimately recovered from a pit-like cattle trap holding an enraged bull. He had been gored and trampled.

The unusual circumstances advanced a variety of theories ranging from accident to suicide. Kenneth

Favrholdt, a Kamloops museum curator who has been researching the life and travels of David Douglas, believes that foul play cannot be ruled out. He visited the stone cairn that marks the site of Douglas's death on the Parker Ranch in Hawaii. At the museum there, Favrholdt was greeted with stony silence when he tried to discuss local lore, which suggests that the night before he was killed Douglas camped with an Australian convict who may have been his murderer.

Embued with a curiosity and enthusiasm for what he called the "great operations of nature," Douglas's contribution to the world of botany is evident today in gardens all over the world where species of lily, phlox and lupine bloom.

"There is scarcely a spot deserving the name of a garden in which some of the discoveries of David Douglas do not form the chief attraction," noted one twentieth-century horticulturist. "To no single individual is modern horticulture more indebted."

TO WALK WITH GIANTS

Cape Breton, Nova Scotia, 1849 — In 1976, American comedian Mel Brooks told CBC's *As It Happens* host Barbara Frum his opinion of Canadians. "I think they are taller than Americans," he said, "they are kinder and they are more gentle." In the case of Nova Scotia's Angus McAskill, he was quite correct.

Young Angus grew up on a Cape Breton farm near St. Ann's Harbour where the McAskill family settled in 1831. They came from Harris in the Hebridean Islands of Scotland and joined a community of expatriate Highlanders in the district called "Englishtown" because its inhabitants did not speak Gaelic.

As a child, Angus was the same size as other boys but when he entered his teens he went off the growing curve. At fourteen, he was well over six feet tall and earned the nickname "Big Boy." Stories about his size and strength spread through the community. After one incident in which he knocked an antagonist unconscious at a dance, he was seldom challenged and became known for his "mild and gentle manner."

By the time Angus reached his twenties, the timber-framed McAskill house was too short for him. The roof and ground floor ceilings were raised, although he still had to duck through the front doorway. The feather or straw mattress on his eight-foot-long bed was lashed with ropes instead of a spring, and eventually even it proved too small.

Angus's strength proved a boon to his family. If a horse went lame ploughing in the field, he could take its place in the traces. One winter night when a "ceilidh" (at home) featuring music and dancing was scheduled, he was driving a team of oxen home with a load of firewood and found them too slow. So he unyoked them to find their own way and pulled the wood himself.

When he wasn't helping to clear the bush and plant the fields, Angus was a fisherman. His boat was ballasted before the mast to accommodate his weight at the stern. Onlookers marvelled when he single-handedly set the forty-foot mast. He never had to bail his half-ton boat, since he could simply set it on the beam and spill out the bilge water. Pranksters once urged him to pull on the bow of the boat while they secretly hauled back and the dory was torn apart in the tug-of-war.

At maturity, Angus was seven feet nine inches tall and weighed 425 pounds. Well-proportioned, he had curly dark hair, deep blue eyes and his voice was described as musical but hollow-sounding.

Although he was content with his life in Englishtown, crop failures and a freak late spring frost in 1848 wreaked hardship on the community and the McAskills. When a Yankee skipper and entrepreneur offered to tour "the big giant" as a curiosity, Angus accepted in hopes of helping his family.

Between 1849 and 1854, Angus was exhibited throughout Lower Canada, the United States, Europe, the West Indies and Cuba. Apocryphal tales abound about his adventures in the American West where he is said to have scared off train robbers by standing in the aisle. Likewise, in an audience with Queen Victoria at Windsor castle, McAskill tradition holds that he was presented with numerous gifts, including a Highland costume and two gold rings. During his Cuban tour, he was nicknamed "Mount Kaskill."

Wearing a cutaway coat trimmed with velvet and a Parisian-made beaver hat with a circumference of twenty-six and a half inches, Angus accepted the stares of the curious, performing exercises while they gawked. His weight-lifting demonstrations were often accompanied by wagering. In one notable instance, he was challenged to lift a 2,700-pound anchor on a wharf that some say was in New York and others place as New Orleans. He successfully executed the press lift, but his grip slipped and the fluke caught his shoulder pinning him beneath it.

When he returned to Cape Breton at twenty-nine, Angus found the area transformed. Many of the families he had grown up with had emigrated to New Zealand with Reverend Norman MacLeod in one of the most bizarre mass exoduses this country has ever seen. More than 850 self-described "Sea Birds" had departed St. Ann's to find a better life half a world away.

Undeterred, Angus used the "snug fortune" he had earned to open a general store across from his parent's home near the shore. The building was constructed to suit his size, and his stool was a 140-gallon molasses puncheon. He also bought a grist mill across the bay, where his strength was used by rolling the millwheels as though they were cookies. The first commercial salmon fishery at St. Ann's is also credited to his enterprise.

Much of his business was conducted in barter and he was known as a fair and friendly merchant who never refused to help a person in need. In his store, Angus sold tea by the pound or by the fistful, and tea from his foot-long palm was the best deal by far.

When he died in his thirty-ninth year after a brief illness diagnosed as "brain fever," the gentle giant of Cape Breton was mourned on a scale proportionate to his size. His gravesite overlooking the harbour has become a popular attraction for tourists, and artifacts from his life are displayed at the Gaelic College of Celtic Arts and Crafts at St. Ann's. By all accounts, he was Mel Brooks's epitome of a Canadian — tall, gentle and kind.

Subsequently, two other Canadians whose size made them notable became the subject of exhibition. Anna Swan of Mill Brook, Nova Scotia was sixteen when she attracted the attention of American showman P.T. Barnum. He touted her as "the tallest girl in the world" and advertised her height at eight foot one inch although she was seven foot six in reality. In 1871, she married Martin Van Buren Bates, a Kentucky-born giant who was three and a half inches shorter. They were billed as "the tallest married couple in the world." Anna bore two children, an eighteen-pound girl who died at birth, and a boy weighing twenty-three pounds twelve ounces, who succumbed after eleven hours.

In Saskatchewan, Edouard Beaupré was known as "the Willow Bunch Giant," after the town where he was born in 1881. Described as "shy, intelligent and tranquil," Edouard was the eldest of twenty children and he grew at a normal rate for the first few years of his life. However, at age nine he was six feet tall and at the peak of his growth he was an awesome eight foot two.

Edouard toured North America on the freak show circuit and relatives accused his agent of keeping the young man drunk and depriving him of his earnings. While performing in the Barnum and Bailey Circus at the St. Louis World Fair in 1904, he suffered a pulmonary hemorrhage and died. His embalmed body was displayed in Montreal and ended up at the University of Montreal where it was used for medical research.

By 1967 the *Canadian Medical Association Journal* reported that the deteriorating corpse had withered to seven foot one. The Beaupré family, who had been unable to recover Edouard's body initially, demanded "respect for his body — and his soul." In 1990 the university returned his remains to Willow Bunch, where the body was cremated. A statue dedicated to the giant was unveiled at a family reunion eighty-six years and three days after his death.

For the record, the tallest human being recorded to date was Robert Pershing Wadlow who stood one-tenth of an inch taller than eight foot eleven inches. He was an American.

A McASKILL PROPORTION SAMPLER
- Height — 7' 9"
- Width of Shoulders — 44"
- Weight — 425 lbs.
- Width of Palm — 8"
- Length of Palm — 12"
- Boot Length — 17 1/2"

NO PRISON IN THE WOODS

Windsor, Canada West, 1852 — The perception of the life that settlers could expect in Canada was often dramatically different. When English "gentlewoman" Susanna Moodie's book *Roughing It in the Bush* was published in 1852, the author noted that her "melancholy narrative" was written "in the hope of deterring well-educated people" from settling "in the Backwoods." In contrast, that same year another woman — a Quaker-educated teacher — published a twelve-page pamphlet recommending emigration.

"No settled country in America offers stronger inducements to coloured people," said the pamphlet. "The general tone of society is healthy, and there is increasing anti-slavery sentiment."

What Susanna Moodie described bleakly as "the green prison of the woods," represented freedom and hope to Mary Ann Shadd, author of "Notes of Canada West."

A freeborn black American, Shadd was twenty-nine when she came to Windsor, Canada West in 1851. The eldest child of a prominent black abolitionist, Abraham Doras Shadd, Mary Ann grew up in Wilmington, Delaware. After attending a Pennsylvania boarding school, she organized her first school for black children when she was sixteen. Constantly involved in anti-slavery initiatives, she viewed education as a tool for black independence and self-respect.

President Millard Fillmore signed the Fugitive Slave Act in 1850. It allowed slave owners the right to reclaim their runaway "property" and subjected abolitionist workers in the "Underground railroad" to fines or imprisonment. Thousands of blacks crossed into Canada, landing everywhere from Saltspring Island on the West Coast to the heartland of southern Ontario in Raleigh Township where a former Louisiana landowner, Reverend William King, established a colony for refugees.

Mary Ann Shadd wanted to help black emigrants adapt to this new environment. Although slavery had been officially abolished in British Empire colonies in 1834, Shadd also felt her mission was "to inculcate a healthy anti-slavery sentiment in a country which, though under British rule, is particularly exposed, by intercommunication, to pro-slavery, religious and secular influence."

Provincial legislation passed in Canada West in 1850 laid the groundwork for segregated schools.

Blacks began establishing their own private school, while continuing to protest the poor quality of education their children could obtain in common schools. One Hamilton-area protester suggested that children left such schools "knowing but a little more about the grammar of their language, than a horse does about handling a musket."

In the autumn of 1851, Mary Ann Shadd was hired by the black community to conduct a school in a ramshackle building that had once been a Windsor barracks. Attendance was lower than expected and some students could not afford even the most modest fee which was to be paid toward their teacher's salary.

The American Missionary Association stepped in to guarantee Shadd an annual salary of $125. After a shaky start, which was aggravated by a cholera epidemic, approximately two dozen pupils were enrolled. Shadd taught all ten classes, covering everything from botany to mathematics. Her pupils ranged in age from four to forty-five.

During the same period, Shadd became embroiled in a controversy involving another black abolitionist and his wife.

Henry Bibb was the son of a white father and a slave mother. Born in Kentucky, he has been described as a "discontented slave" and was reportedly sold for figures ranging from $350 to $1,200 before escaping and fleeing to the North. Bibb and his second wife, Mary, settled in Sandwich (near Windsor).

In January, 1851, Henry began publishing *The Voice of the Fugitive*, the first black newspaper published in Upper Canada. At the same time, Mary opened a school. To all intents, the Bibbs' goals and Shadd's seemed to be syncopated.

However, along with newspaper and his work in the Canadian Anti-Slavery Society, Henry Bibb also founded the Refugee Home Society. The RHS collected donations to purchase land for refugees. Shadd denounced this as "begging," and ultimately accused Bibb of fraud. It seems that some of the land acquired never found its way to fugitive ownership and "agents" who collected the funds kept as much as 63 percent for themselves.

Although she described it as a painful duty, Shadd denounced Bibb to the American Missionary Association. "It is no slander to say that Henry Bibb has hundreds of dollars belonging to fugitives, probably thousands would be nearer the truth," she wrote. "Henry Bibb is a dishonest man, and as such must be known to the world." She expressed disappointment at the situation "involving as it does loss of confidence, in coloured men, who assume to be leaders of their people."

Bibb struck back at Shadd in the pages of *The Voice of the Fugitive*, accusing her of concealing funds she was receiving from the American Missionary Association. Shadd was also falsely accused of refusing to accept white children at her school, even though her views on integration as a means of ensuring that blacks were not ghettoized were well known. Ultimately, the AMA withdrew Shadd's funding. In a letter to the association Shadd said: "This whole business is really sickening to me."

On March 24, 1853, the first issue of the *Provincial Freeman* was published. Well-known American abolitionist Samuel Ringold Ward was listed as the editor of the weekly newspaper "Devoted to Anti-Slavery, Temperance and General Literature," but that was simply a ruse to boost circulation. Mary Shadd was the functioning editor, and as such became the first black woman on the continent to found and edit a newspaper. After one issue, publication was suspended while Shadd spent a year raising money through a lecture tour.

The *Provincial Freeman* resumed publication in Toronto in 1854. The paper's motto was "Self-Reliance is the True Road to Independence." In the *Freeman*, Shadd discussed all aspects of the black experience in Canada, exposing bigotry and decrying compromises on slavery. She opposed any notion of second-class status and urged blacks to assimilate rather than isolate themselves in self-segregated communities.

Publication was somewhat sporadic and in 1855 the paper moved to Chatham, Ontario under a new editor. That year, Shadd became the first woman to speak at the National Negro Convention, where she earned the admiration of activist Frederick Douglass.

In 1856, Mary married a black businessman, Thomas Fauntleroy Cary. They had a son in 1858, but Cary died before the birth of their daughter in 1861. The *Freeman* continued publishing until 1859, with Mary serving as one of three editors and her sister, Amelia, and brother, Isaac, assisting. Their father, Abraham, became the first black man to hold public office when he was elected to the town council of Raleigh Township.

Whether she was meeting with John Brown while he plotted his rebellion in Chatham or wrenching a child away from slave-hunters, Shadd remained at the centre of black politics and social assimilation.

When the Civil War broke out, she returned to the United States to serve as an enlistment recruitment officer. After the war, she resumed her teaching career in Washington, D.C., returning to Canada briefly to organize a suffragist rally.

At forty-six, she became the first woman law student at John Howard University, but she was not granted her degree until 1883 due to sexual discrimination. In America she crusaded for women's rights to vote alongside Susan B. Anthony and Elizabeth Cady Stanton, and testified before the Judiciary Committee of the House of Representatives. She holds the distinction of being the first black woman to vote in a national election.

The citation inducting Mary Ann Shadd Cary into the National Women's Hall of Fame at Seneca Falls,

New York in 1998 concludes: "As an educator, an abolitionist, an editor, an attorney and a feminist, she dedicated her life to improving the quality of life for everyone — black and white, male and female."

They might have added "American and Canadian."

THE COLOUR OF THE OLD WEST

Highwood River, Alberta, 1882 — John Ware was born into slavery on a plantation in South Carolina in 1845, the second youngest of eleven children. Reports say that he had never worn shoes until he was twenty years old and he never learned to read or write. But John Ware knew how to sit a horse and rope a steer. Most importantly, he knew how to make his acquaintance with whites work to his peaceable advantage.

By the time the Civil War ended and American blacks were freed from slavery, Ware was living in Texas and refining his skills as a cowboy. Black cowboys were not unknown in the American West, but the Canadian West was another matter entirely.

In 1882, Ware joined a cattle drive from Idaho, where Alberta's "King of Canadian Cattle Trails," Tom Lynch, was waiting to escort 3,000 head of foundation stock to the North-West Cattle Company (later known as the Bar U) in the foothills southwest of Calgary on the Highwood River.

"Trailing" was everything and more than the Old West fantasies produced by Hollywood. Six skilled cowboys could handle 1,000 cattle, and every cowboy travelled with at least half a dozen horses. There was always a chuckwagon, a cook to complain about and a trail boss to hear the complaints. It was hard work to move a large herd even nineteen kilometres (twelve miles) a day. Cowboys stayed in the saddle morning to dusk supervising the "doggies."

Tom Lynch was looking for experienced cowhands to drive the herd. John Ware's name kept coming up, but Lynch is said to have hesitated at the notion of hiring a "Negro," until at least one cowboy said he wouldn't take the job unless Ware was along. Ware was assigned to a clunker of a horse and a junker of a saddle. He started the drive at the "drag end" of the herd, where there was the most dust and dirt on a dry day and the muckiest mud on a wet one.

When the herd reached its destination, John Ware was riding at the front of the herd on a horse the other cowboys had considered a handsome outlaw. And he was sitting in a comfortable saddle. Assuming that a former plantation slave would have little horse savvy, Lynch had made an entertainment out of a request Ware had made for a sturdier animal and more supple seating. Instead of falling off the wild and bucking horse as anticipated, Ware had ridden his outlaw mount to a standstill. When he accepted his pay, Ware was asked to stay on at the ranch.

Ware stayed at the Bar U for several years before hiring on at the Quorn ranch on Sheep Creek. The purpose of the Quorn was rather unusual. It was funded by The Quorn Hunt Club of Leicestershire, England, and its primary purpose was to raise hunter horses for the British market. Several hundred hunter-type mares and twenty thoroughbred and Cleveland Bay stallions were imported as foundation stock. Raising cattle was just a sideline.

While Ware did not participate in the Quorn events such as rugger, cricket and riding to hounds, he did earn the respect of the English for his uncanny horsemanship.

In 1885, a huge general round-up was held in the spring. One hundred cowboys combed the foothills, rounding up 60,000 cattle. The Quorn sent John Ware as its representative.

"If there is a man on the round-up who keeps up the spirits of the boys more than another and provides amusement to break the monotony, this man is John Ware," declared the June 23, 1885, Macleod *Gazette*. "The horse is not running on the prairie which John cannot ride."

Over the years, Ware acquired the nucleus of a cattle herd of his own, sometimes taking an animal in lieu of wages. In 1890, he started his own small ranching operation on the north shore of Sheep Creek. His brand was 9999, which was said to be his lucky number. Biographer Grant MacEwan called the Four

Nines or "walking-stick" brand "hideous." Later, Ware reduced it to three nines, which charred slightly less cowhide.

In 1892, John met Mildred Lewis, whose father was a Calgary carpenter. Lightning struck, quite literally, while they were courting. A bolt killed the two horses that were pulling the buggy in which John had taken Mildred for a country ride. Tall, strong John pulled the rig back to town. Shortly afterwards, the pair were married.

Black American cowboy Bill Pickett is credited with inventing the sport of steer wrestling, but newly-wed John Ware earned the distinction of being the first to demonstrate it in Canada at a Calgary fair. He learned the skill defending himself against a longhorn cow that charged a group of cowboys in a corral. Ware grabbed the enraged bovine by the horns. While she dragged him around, he managed to wrap an arm around her muzzle and pulled her to the ground by the nose until she fell under his control. At the Calgary steer roping and tying competition, it took Ware fifty-one seconds to immobilize a steer. He won $100 and a new saddle.

John and Mildred began raising a family. They appear to have integrated comfortably into the community. On one occasion Ware was apparently taunted by racist remarks in a Calgary tavern. He knocked the offender out and then graciously took him to a hospital and paid the doctor's bill.

When a Medicine Hat hotel tried to refuse him a room, Ware's friends stood up for him and "set the hotel man straight." Although he was known throughout his life as "Nigger John," even the *Canadian Encyclopedia* goes to lengths to point out that this "was not intended pejoratively."

The mythology of John Ware's abilities with animals grew to the proportion of legend. It has been said that he could walk across the backs of a corral filled with bulls, run faster than a three-year-old steer, and leap into a saddle without touching a stirrup. The only thing he could not countenance was snakes.

The Sheep Creek area began filling up with settlers after the completion of the railway from Calgary to Fort Macleod. Ware had 300 head of cattle and he needed more grazing room, so he sold his ranch for $1,000 and moved northeast to Brooks on the Red Deer River.

In the spring of 1905, Mildred Ware died of typhoid and pneumonia despite John's efforts to obtain medicine for her during a freak blizzard. Their five young children grew up with relatives. At least two of the boys served in World War I, but afterwards the only work they could find was as railway porters.

Tragedy struck John Ware a few months after Mildred's death. He was killed when his horse tripped and fell on him after stepping into a badger hole. The Calgary Public Library's website tribute to Ware as a hero of the Old West contains this curious bit of trivia:

"A young lawyer named R.B. Bennett was assigned to handle Ware's estate. Cowboys laughed at Bennett's folly of selling all of Ware's horses and then having to rent horses to round up Ware's cattle. Bennett is the only Canadian Prime Minister to have lived and worked in Calgary."

At the funeral, a Baptist minister called John Ware "one of God's most cheerful children" and noted that, "He convinced me that black is a beautiful colour. . . . His example and message on brotherhood should be entrenched in our hearts."

Five years after Ware's death, 1,000 blacks from Oklahoma attempted to move to the Edmonton area but they were thwarted by public hostility against what one politician called "Dark Spots."

The Edmonton *Capital* carried a Board of Trade petition that stated: "We submit that the advent of such negroes as are here now was most unfortunate for the country, and that further arrivals in large numbers would be disastrous."

An order-in-council from the federal government barred black immigration for one year. It was ultimately withdrawn, only to be replaced by more subtle means of discouraging black immigration, including utilizing immigration agents who travelled the United States spreading the word in black communities that the climate was cold and agricultural prospects limited.

SIR BARTON
AND THE COMMANDER

Windsor, Ontario, 1920 — It was billed as "The Race of the Century." Two stallions would meet in Windsor, Ontario before a crowd estimated at 30,000 to determine who was the fastest horse of all.

Representing the United States was the great Man o' War, who had won nineteen out of twenty races and had been voted the "Three-Year-Old of the Year."

Canadian hopes were on another chestnut horse, Sir Barton, the first winner of racing's Triple Crown, owned by Montreal millionaire Commander John Kenneth Levenson Ross.

Commander Ross was one of the most flamboyant characters ever seen in Canadian horse racing. Born in Lindsay, Ontario, he was the son of railway baron, James Ross, who earned his fortune as one of the "Big Four" who blasted the Canadian Pacific Railway through the Rocky Mountains. The same vigour his father applied to making money, his son applied to spending it.

An only son, Ross was educated at Bishop's College School in Lennoxville, Quebec and earned a Bachelor of Science degree from McGill University, where he was best-known as a star lineman on the football team. While the father was grooming the heir apparent in matters of business, the son took time out to learn sleight-of-hand card tricks and delighted in producing an ace of spades from the left ear of any new acquaintance.

As the assistant general manager of the Dominion Coal Company, which his father purchased in 1901, Ross divided his time between head office in Montreal and the mines in Sydney, Nova Scotia. At his summer home in Cape Breton, he devoted himself largely to sailing his seventy-five-foot yacht and fishing for world-record tuna.

Ross's father died in 1913, leaving an estate estimated at sixteen million dollars, which his son would inherit when he turned forty in 1916. In the interim, the will provided a generous annual allowance of $75,000 and allowed Ross to use up to one million dollars for purposes of business or property acquisition. Ross seems to have interpreted this liberally, using it to acquire a 106-foot, custom-built motor yacht.

When the First World War broke out, Ross loaned the yacht to the sadly undershipped Canadian navy and donated $500,000 to the government toward the war effort. In the early days of the war, he bought two more steam yachts and gave them to the navy.

Ross served on one, *Grilse*, as a reserve lieutenant and commanded the ship on patrols between Halifax and Bermuda for two years. Then the government seconded him to serve as Chairman of the Dominion Board of Pension Commissioners. In 1917, the navy promoted Ross to the rank of commander in recognition of his generous contributions.

Ross began acquiring race horses in 1914. Two years later, he built a million-dollar breeding stable at Verchères on the St. Lawrence River. The barns were painted in his racing colours — black and orange — and he had a string of nearly fifty horses.

Once the operation was in full swing, Ross was known to ferry his friends to racetracks in his private railway car. He was also known for his bold wagers.

In 1918, a front-page headline in a Chicago sporting journal reported that a Canadian navy officer had bet $50,000 on a horse named Canso and parlayed the winning bet into a million dollars.

The New York Jockey Club reportedly asked Commander Ross to ease up.

That same summer, Ross bought a winless, American-bred, two-year-old colt named Sir Barton for $10,000. Samuel Riddle of Philadelphia paid half that amount for an awkward colt named Man o' War.

The first Canadian owner to win the Kentucky Derby was not in attendance on the day of the 1919 run for the roses. Ross was in Toronto attending his dying father-in-law when Sir Barton led the field of twelve by five lengths for the win. Another Ross Stable horse, Billy Kelly, finished second. Then four days later, Sir Barton won the Preakness Stakes at Baltimore.

For a horse who had never won a race before, whose hooves were so "shelly" (brittle) that he could lose four shoes in a race, Sir Barton was on a prestigious winning streak. That June he won the Belmont Stakes in a three-horse race. Although now recognized as the first winner of racing's "Triple Crown," the designation and trophy for Sir Barton's achievement was not created until several decades later.

Commander Ross cleared more than half a million dollars in 1918 and 1919 between the purses his horses won and the bets he successfully wagered. He established a second breeding farm in Maryland and became one of the top winning owners in America.

In 1920, the racing world clamoured for a match race between Sir Barton and the sensational Man o' War. American racetracks vied to host the spectacle, but Kenilworth Park in Windsor won the day by offering the largest payday racing had ever seen at the time — a $75,000 purse to the winner. General admission tickets were five dollars a piece.

On the afternoon of October 12, the two horses met. Man o' War was a year younger than Sir Barton and he was the crowd's betting favourite.

Sir Barton had the rail position and for a brief instant at the start of the race his head was even with the rangy stallion that was affectionately known to America as "Big Red."

Alas, the day did not belong to Sir Barton.

He finished seven lengths behind Man o' War, who broke the track record by six seconds even though his jockey had him on a tight rein.

Man o' War retired to stud after the race. Sir Barton never regained his stature as a winner. He, too, was put out to stud, but he failed to sire any notable winners.

The only Canadian-owned horse to win the Triple Crown was shuffled off to the breeding shed at a U.S. cavalry remount farm, where his fee was a measly ten dollars. Sir Barton died in 1937 and he is remembered every year at Pimlico Raceway in a stakes race named in his honour.

Like his stallion, Commander Ross faced setbacks in the years that followed the race. He spent lavishly, remodelling his forty-room mansion on Peel Street in Montreal and holding a "house-warming" party that included the Duke of Windsor, who was then the Prince of Wales. But the expenses of horse racing, the maintenance of the breeding farms, the thirty or more servants, the seven or eight Rolls-Royces and all of the yachts began taking their toll. What he later termed "unwise investments" led to Ross's bankruptcy in 1928.

It seems Ross had fallen into the thrall of an American promoter and financier who had involved him in vastly unprofitable investments in oil. "I had never seen an oil field in my life. I don't pretend to know anything about oil or oil wells," he told a meeting of his creditors.

A story in the Montreal *Star* headlined "Most Regrettable Local Insolvency," described Ross as "victimized by designing people," and recounted his many philanthropic contributions. In a dozen years, Ross managed to whittle his sixteen-million-dollar legacy to $300 in cash.

Fortuitously, a codicil in his father's will had set up a trust fund of one million dollars to provide income for Ross during his lifetime and later for his two children.

With a guaranteed income of at least $50,000 a year, the former millionaire was able to live comfortably on a sunny estate in Montego Bay, Jamaica, which was later sold to another flamboyant Canadian millionaire, Max Aitken (Lord Beaverbrook).

Commander J.K.L. Ross died, horseless, in 1951.

THESE BOOTS
WERE MADE FOR WALKIN'

Halifax to Vancouver, 1921 — It might not be everyone's idea of a stroll, but in the middle of the winter of
1921 Charles Burkman decided to walk across the
country. He was twenty years old and he had just lost
his job at the Halifax shipyards. An acquaintance, Sid
Carr, was also out of work. The footloose pair formu-
lated an equally loose plan to tred the railway tracks
west until something better came along or they waded
into the Pacific.

When they announced their plans to the Halifax
Herald, the adventurers anticipated the trip would
take seven months at a leisurely pace. Along the way,
they planned to sell commemorative postcards for a
dime, a princely sum considering that a turkey dinner
cost about twenty cents.

The *Herald* must have been having a slow news
year. Seizing on the story as though it was "news,"

they offered to pay for reports and made Charlie and Sid front-page news.

On January 17, Pathé News filmed the duo's departure in fog and rain, but no one guessed how big the story would get.

As they walked, a pattern emerged involving free meals, lodging and gifts of everything from boots to long johns. Hundreds of postcard-buying well-wishers offered them encouragement and they plodded on despite freezing temeperatures. But on January 21, they had competition.

John Behan, a forty-four-year-old postman from Dartmouth, proposed a father-son challenge. He told the *Herald* that he and his twenty-four-year-old son, Clifford, could reach Vancouver in six months. Burkman and Carr had a nine-day advantage by the time they set out, but team Behan proclaimed that they would be in the lead by Montreal. Carrying their own stash of commemorative postcards, the Behans gave hot pursuit. They were at Truro composing their own dispatches to the *Herald* when a third team of hikers threw their soles in the ring.

Windsor, Nova Scotia foundry worker Frank Dill and his wife, Jennie, added a whole new dimension. Married less than two years, they both enjoyed the outdoors and Frank had earned a modest reputation as a runner.

Dark-haired, diminutive Jennie was the wild card. A muscular fisherman's daughter, she was a good shot and a notable speed skater. Joining the race was her idea and she created a sensation by wearing men's clothing — riding breeches and high leather boots. The *Herald* dutifully noted that there was "not a single suggestion of mannishness in her personality."

Before the Dills got started on February 1, Sid Carr dropped out. "I won't be forced into racing across Canada," he told the press, who promptly romanticized Charles Burkman as "the lone hiker."

Two thousand Haligonians saw the Dills off in a heavy snowfall. That day, Burkman crossed into Maine and the Behans were gaining ground on him near Saint John. Although doubters argued no woman could hike beyond Truro, Jennie Dill's report from Truro said that she hoped to walk past Moncton the following day, "if Frank can stand it."

Wagering on the outcome became frenetic. Despite offers of rides in everything from sleighs to railway cars, the contestants kept walking.

Halifax businessmen sympathetic to Burkman's solitary plight pledged $500 if he reached Vancouver in six months. Meanwhile, three wildcats attacked the Behans and John shot one of them. Although huge crowds turned out to shower the Dills with notes, newspapers and food, Jenny never let Frank slow the pace.

Burkman had gone through sixteen changes of boots when he reached Montreal on February 19. He stayed at the swank Windsor Hotel, delighting

Montrealers by dancing all evening despite his blisters.

At the end of February, Burkman had travelled 1,490 kilometres (926 miles) in forty-two days. The Behans were hard on his heels, clocking 1,382 kilometres (859 miles) in thirty-four days. Despite waist-high snow in Maine, the Dills made 928 kilometres (577 miles) in twenty- two days.

In Halifax, a $1,000 bet was placed that the Behans would overtake Burkman by March 12. The Dills hardly seemed to be in contention.

Father and son Behan walked the snowy rails with a pole held between them to help keep their balance. Jennie was small and Frank was tall, so they could not effect the same device. Somewhere between North Bay and Sudbury, Burkman found a roller skate. Tied to a spanning rod, it ran on the opposite rail and Charlie balanced against it. On March 12, he was only a few hours ahead of the Behans. Someone lost $1,000.

Two days later, the Burkman–Behan paths crossed in the depths of Northern Ontario. They spent that day walking together, a pleasurable respite for Burkman, whose only dialogue with human company usually occurred when he was exhausted after a day's hike. For the rest of the month, the two teams engaged in a foot duel — sometimes gaining, sometimes losing ground by trying false shortcuts — but the Behans were the first to reach Lake Superior.

Way back in Ottawa, the Dills enjoyed a meeting with Prime Minister Arthur Meighen and Liberal leader William Lyon Mackenzie King. Jennie thrilled readers with news that she had killed a timber wolf with a single shot after it leapt out of the bushes at Frank. They were picking up the pace despite heavy storms and white-out conditions.

Sometimes the newspaper would not hear from Burkman for days, but he was always dogging the Behans. In sub-zero temperatures north of Superior, they spent several days walking together. Wolves howled at the door of a cabin where they took shelter.

Port Arthur (now Thunder Bay) was Burkman's hometown, so he stopped to spend some time. The Behans savoured their lead; crossing the halfway point at Savanne, Ontario they were "feeling like two jack rabbits." Jennie Dill titillated the nation by suggesting that her husband was jealous of letters she received from Charlie Burkman and thought that the lonely hiker might be slowing down so that he could walk with her. Burkman had slowed down, but only because he hurt his hip slipping off a rail.

Warm weather brought its own strains. Frank Dill suffered from sunburn, while Burkman opted to walk at night to avoid the heat. Despite heat waves, mosquitos and prairie sandstorms, the hikers made good time on the flat land.

Blisters slowed Burkman down. When the Dills overtook him, Jenny said she was sorry but he would have to take care of himself. Noting that "this wonderful hike" had taught her a lesson she intended to share with other women, she wrote: "The subject is not what men can do women can do, but what men have done women CAN MORE THAN DO."

What Jennie Dill could not do was prevent Frank from carousing with friends in Calgary. The Behans were barely two days ahead and she was furious when Frank "went out with the boys." After hauling him out of the Kiwanis Club in the late afternoon, they walked sixteen kilometres (ten miles) in a hailstorm before stopping.

In the Rockies, John and Clifford Behan suffered nosebleeds. John had lost almost 10 percent of his bodyweight and Clifford caught a chill sleeping outdoors at Lake Louise. When a painful spasm stopped him at Albert Canyon, Clifford took a train west to Revelstoke for a prescribed rest. Returning to Albert Canyon, he resumed the hike toward his father, who reached Revelstoke in the interim.

Charlie Burkman was effectively out of the race but he decided to stick it out, acknowledging that, "Some might criticize me for letting a woman pass me."

Jennie Dill was pushing Frank hard, even though his feet were bothering him. At one point outside of Kamloops she accused the Behans of cheating so that they would not be beaten by a woman. The charge could not be substantiated.

On June 11, after walking twenty-two hours straight covering a remarkable 98 kilometres (61 miles), the haggard Behans arrived in Vancouver. Two days later, the Dills followed and Jennie reportedly "looked more as if she had been on a picnic." Burkman joined them on July 16.

In the end, the Dills were the winners. They had travelled the 5,872 kilometres (3,650 miles) in 134 days, bettering the Behans by two days. At 150 days, Charlie Burkman outdid his original "leisurely paced" estimate by two months, but the promised $500 never materialized.

There was no pot of gold at the end of the rainbow. In Monopoly terms, the Trans-Canada hikers simply passed "Go" and started at zero. That July, an attempt at a high-stakes footrace with John, Frank and Charlie foundered when one dropped out and the others suffered heat prostration. They were finished as "news" and dropped from public view.

Ultimately, the notion of walking the country enjoyed its finest hour in 1980, when a youthful, one-legged victim of cancer named Terry Fox announced plans to make his way from Newfoundland to his home province of British Columbia.

Terry's unforgettable "Marathon of Hope" ended tragically in Thunder Bay when doctors diagnosed that the cancer had spread to his lungs. He died the following summer, leaving a legacy of courage that resounds to this day in the annual "runs" that are held in his name, raising millions to fight the disease that challenged him to greatness.

LADYLIKE AND LETHAL

Ottawa, 1947 — It might seem a circuitous route from the badminton court to the politicized arena of consumer advocacy, but Dorothy McKenzie Walton was both a world-class badminton player and a leading force in the Canadian Association of Consumers. On and off the court, she had a confident stride and she never took her eye off the "birdie."

When she was a student at the University of Saskatchewan during the 1920s, Swift Current–born Dorothy was known as "the girl with the million-dollar smile." She excelled in athletics, participating in everything from hockey to the high jump. A member of fourteen intercollegiate sports teams, she was the first woman to qualify for the university's top athletic honour, the Oak Shield.

An above-average student, Dorothy was also the only female member of the university debating team, a team which won the Western championships and out-pointed the English and Australians. Years later, as a sought-after public speaker, she summed up her technique: "Have something to say, say it and shut up."

Her father, Edmund, was a successful merchant and a leading local Liberal. The only hint of rebellion Dorothy seems to have exhibited in her youth was participating in a Conservative election campaign when she was seventeen. She said she did it to get out of the family "rut."

Between 1924 and her marriage to Toronto businessman Bill Walton in 1931, Dorothy won more than fifty provincial and Western Canadian tennis titles and several badminton titles. She also earned a Masters degree. Her thesis was on Canadian immigration.

After giving birth to a son, John, Dorothy began playing badminton in earnest. By 1939, she had won every major singles title in North America, along with numerous mixed doubles titles and a half-dozen tennis titles. She was thirty years old when she travelled to England to participate in the World's Amateur championship.

Even though Great Britain was the cradle of the game — the Duke of Bedford having named it after his country estate, Badminton House, in the late nineteenth century — the British would have done well to be wary of this racquet-carrying Canadian. In 1930, four top British players had been roundly trounced by Guelph, Ontario's Jack Purcell. Dorothy Walton proceeded to duplicate the feat.

"Mrs. Walton achieved Number One ranking because of a rare combination of abilities," wrote S.F. Wise and Douglas Fisher in *Canada's Sporting Heroes*. "The intelligence and deception of her play, especially at the net and in the production of beautifully paced, tantalisingly soft drop shots, enabled her to seize and hold the psychological edge that gives mastery in any sport."

At the top of her game, Walton's athletic career was cut off by the Second World War. In 1940, she was the runner-up for the Lou Marsh Trophy, an oversight that sports historians have attributed to the lack of publicity granted badminton. A decade later the Canadian Press hailed her as one of the top Canadian female athletes of the half-century.

Birds and racquets were in short supply throughout the war and Walton restricted her play to exhibition games for the troops. More importantly, she was involved with a variety of wartime initiatives, including the Wartime Prices and Trades Board (WPTB).

The idea of a consumer group sprang up after the war. A survey conducted by the National Council of Women showed that 80 percent of Canadian women favoured continuing the information flow about products that had started with the WPTB.

In 1947, a handful of women, including Dorothy Walton, approached the government for funding to bring together fifty-six women's organizations from across Canada.

The meeting took place in Ottawa. It was a curious combination of clubwomen and housewives. There were representatives of political, business and professional associations and church groups, including the matronly leader of the Salvation Army and an opinionated Communist.

While Lady Ishbel Aberdeen's founding meeting of the National Women's Council in 1893 floundered initially over controversy concerning the opening prayer, this meeting was all business.

A constitution was drafted and dues were set at fifty cents. The all-woman Canadian Association of Consumers was launched with the motto: "In unity there is strength."

Early initiatives dealt with everyday issues. For example, clothing sizes varied enormously. A woman who thought she wore a size twelve dress might purchase the same size from another manufacturer and find that it required substantial alteration. The sizing of children's clothing was mind-bogglingly stupid.

In 1949 the CAC began drafting a universal labelling system for clothes. They discovered that the U.S. army had drawn up a standard measurement system after systematically analyzing millions of male and female figures for the purpose of churning out wartime uniforms. Using this data, the CAC set about standardizing clothing sizes. Then they turned their sights on the textile industry, demanding "true labelling" about the content and care of garments.

Dorothy Walton became president of the CAC in 1950. Whether she was challenging deceptive bacon packaging or lobbying hosiery manufacturers to list the leg length on their product packaging, Walton was unrelenting.

In a 1952 article for *Maclean's* magazine, June Callwood described Dorothy Walton's leadership of the CAC as "a ladylike but lethal warfare against carelessness, fraud, ennui and ignorance in high places."

The CAC persuaded the government to require that soap and detergent manufacturers accurately list the weight of their product. They checked the accuracy of butcher scales and they demanded that a twenty-four-ounce loaf of bread weigh twenty-four ounces.

There was nothing too mundane to escape their concern, whether it was the price of eggs in April or the vitamin content of apple juice. In the Supreme Court of Canada, the CAC argued that a federal ban on margarine violated the British North America Act. They won.

Ralph Nadar was still a teenager in 1953 when Dorothy Walton was awarded the Coronation Medal for her service to the Canadian public. Behind that million-dollar smile Walton maintained a gutsy determination that made her both a champion athlete and a champion of the people.

LILY OF THE MOHAWKS, GENEVIÈVE OF NEW FRANCE

Caughnawaga to Rome, 1980 — "Catherine Tekakwitha, who are you? Are you (1658–1680)? Is that enough? Are you the Iroquois Virgin? Are you the Lily of the Shores of the Mohawk River? Can I love you in my own way?" Thus begins Leonard Cohen's elegiac, controversial, some say pornographic, 1966 novel *Beautiful Losers*, which, among other things, is an evocation of the first Indian saint, Kateri (Catherine) Tekakwitha.

Kateri Tekakwitha was venerated by Pope Pius XII in 1943 and subsequently beatified by Pope John Paul II on June 22, 1980. The history of the Catholic Church in Canada is, like Cohen's novel, controversial, no where more so than in Quebec. But it is a seminal history. The Church was hugely influential in Canada's settlement and its establishment as a nation. In no single story is that influence more confounding, more resonate, than in the story of Kateri Tekakwitha. The daughter of a Christian Algonkin squaw and a pagan Mohawk, Kateri was born in 1656 near what is now Auriesville in Albany, New York State. Her mother had been brought up by French settlers at Trois-Rivières, then captured by the Mohawks around 1653. Instead of being killed, she was taken as a wife and Kateri was conceived.

Along with religion and fire water the Europeans also brought disease to the New World. In 1660 Kateri Tekakwitha's mother succumbed, as did her husband and their last-born child, to a smallpox epidemic. Young Kateri survived, but barely. She was, from then on, an exceedingly frail creature, with badly damaged eyes and a heavily scarred, pockmarked face. Kateri was taken in by her uncle, the first chieftain of the Turtle Clan village called Gandauoque (Caughnawaga). Ironically, her uncle was a vociferous and dedicated enemy of the white man and the Christian faith.

In the fall of 1666 Prouville de Tracy came down from Quebec, burned and plundered these centres of the Mohawk population and their stores. Decimated, the Mohawk begged for peace and dutifully asked for missionaries to placate the maurading French. Three black-robed Jesuit emissaries arrived in Gandauoque in September 1667. During the three days they were there, eleven-year-old Kateri was charged with their care. Whatever happened during those three days, a change came over the young Indian child that not even her avuncular uncle could reverse.

Her piety and refusal to marry, as her relatives frequently tried to arrange for her to do, is not necessarily as miraculous as zealous Catholic chroniclers would have the student of Canadian history believe; two-thirds of the population of Gandauoque was composed of Christian Algonkins and Hurons who undoubtedly proselytized the religious life and spoke to Kateri about the Ursulines of Quebec in glowing terms. Kateri was not without a "support group," in spite of her uncle's disapproval.

Kateri formally converted to Catholicism in 1675. Her conversion brought with it the wrath of her uncle and those in her community who felt as he did. Legend has it that there was active persecution of the young girl — death threats and beatings — all of which left the fragile Kateri physically more challenged but emotionally more resolved.

The priests advised her to pray unrelentingly and if her prayers did not stay the savages, to flee her village and go and live at the mission near Lachine Rapids more than 320 kilometres (200 miles) away. There her faith would be readily accepted.

In the fall of 1677, at the age of twenty-one, with the aid of three Indian neophytes, Kateri fled. It was at the Saint-Francois-Xavier mission at Sault St. Louis near Montreal that Kateri prepared herself for the chaste life as a devout Catholic. Anastasie Tegonhatsiongo, who had been her mother's friend at Osser-nenon (Auriesville, N.Y.), was recruited as Kateri's spiritual guide.

In the spring of 1678, she was received into the Confrérie de la Sainte-Famille (The Holy Family), despite the fact that she was a very young novice. She continued to live the full lndian life, accompanying her people on the great winter hunts, up until the last two years of her life. However, her commitment to chastity and strength of purpose gave the caretaker French priests an impression of exceptional spirituality.

On the feast of the Annunciation, March 25, 1679, she was permitted to take in private the vow of perpetual chastity. Thus neo-Catholic posterity gave her the moniker, Lily of the Mohawks.

As it is obsessively and imaginatively documented in Cohen's novel, Kateri adopted a penitential lifestyle — long periods of enforced silence, fasting, standing in the cold dawn for hours with little protection from the elements, self-mutilation — all of which invariably hastened her early demise a mere three years after her arrival at the mission.

Her sainthood has rightfully met with skepticism, even hostility, by some native peoples and non-Catholics, who contend that an imperialistic Church had co-opted a "Native Person" for its own purposes.

The Catholic Church's Congregation for the Causes of Saints (the Vatican department that attends to the business of selecting and recommending veneration, beatification and canonization to the Pope) puts a priority on candidates who represent occupations or peoples who have no saints to celebrate. Until the twentieth century, the Church had never put a priority on women. Only 20 percent of the saints canonized up to 1900 were female. That number has increased.

It was Kateri Tekakwitha's "pastoral priority" that determined her beatification, despite the fact that all of the miracles attributed to her intercession lacked certification.

The fledgling church in North America was unequipped in the seventeenth century to carry out the formal investigations necessary to establish a miracle's validity, normally a prerequisite for sainthood. According to the French Jesuit historian Father Charlevoix, miracles took place at Kateri's humble tomb, which became a place of pilgrimage for the parishes around Montreal. He recorded a story about a newly arrived parish priest named Father Rémy who refused to lead the annual pilgrimage to Kateri's grave because, the new priest avowed, such worship was not acknowledged by the Church. According to Father Charlevoix's story, the priest fell gravely ill that very day and only recovered when he relented and agreed to lead the procession. Pope John Paul II decided when he made Kateri a saint in 1980 that her reputation for producing miracles was sufficient.

Kateri died on April 17, 1680 at 3 o'clock in the afternoon. Her last words are said to have been "Jesos

Konoronkwa" (Jesus I love you). According to the Jesuit priests who were present fifteen minutes after her death, the ugly pox marks and scars on her face suddenly disappeared and she was made beautiful.

In 1688, Bishop Saint-Vallier, the second bishop of Quebec, declared Kateri "the Geneviève of Canada." In 1744 Father Charlevoix wrote that she was "universally regarded as the Protectress of Canada."

A Joan-of-Arc figure, Kateri's legend grows, nurtured by papal authority. She is a patron saint of exiles, orphans and people ridiculed for their piety. Each year sees more pilgrimages to Auriesville, where the American Catholic Church has built The National Shrine of the North American Martyrs presided over by the Lily of the Mohawks, and to the François-Xavier mission at Caughnawaga where Kateri Tekakwitha's relics are maintained.

INNOVATION
&
INVENTION

THE STORY OF DR. "O"

THE HEART OF THE MATTER

H_2O + MYSTERIOUS GREY POWDER =
SUNSHINE + \$\$\$\$

RUST NEVER SLEEPS

FEETS DON'T FAIL ME NOW

IS IT A BIRD? IS IT A PLANE?
NO, IT'S AN ARROW!

THE STORY OF DR. "O"

Brantford, Ontario, 1860 — Oronhyatekha was one smart Mohawk. From the time he was a young brave on the Six Nations Reserve near Brantford, Ontario in the mid-1800s, he took advantage of every opportunity made available to Reserve Indians by the equivocal benevolence of certain church organizations and the governments of Canada.

Baptized Peter Martin in the Anglican Church, throughout his sixty-six years he insisted that he be called by his Indian name Oronhyatekha, which means "Burning Cloud."

In 1867, he became the first native person to graduate from a university in Canada, and the first accredited native medical doctor.

Previously, Oronhyatekha had studied at Oxford University in England at the invitation of the Prince of Wales, whom he met when the Prince visited the Brantford reserve in 1860.

When Oronhyatekha returned to Canada from England in 1863, he married Ellen Hill, the great-granddaughter of Joseph Brant, and her Indian name, Karakwineh, meant "Moving Sun."

By all accounts, "Moving Sun" and "Burning Cloud" had a wonderful marriage until a son tragically died in 1881. "Moving Sun" then stopped moving and became a virtual recluse. After she died in 1901, Dr. O also went steadily downhill until he succumbed to complications from diabetes in 1907.

But his successful marriage, or the details of his education, his medical degree and the attendant success it brought Oronhyatekha, even the untimely death of his son are not at the core of his story.

Dr. O's story is that of a full-blooded Mohawk Indian who ultimately made a significant career joining white men's fraternal societies typically defined by their racist policies.

As a student at the University of Toronto, he joined the secret order of Freemasons. Later, after practising medicine for a decade, he joined the ultra-Protestant Orangemen and ultimately the Independent Order of Foresters, a fraternal society based on life insurance that claimed its roots in the medieval England and attitude of Robin Hood.

To even be considered for membership in the Independent Order of Foresters, a man had to be a member of the Orange Society.

Founded in Ireland in 1795 to keep alive the memory of the "Glorious Revolution" and the Battle of the Boyne, where the Protestant succession to the British throne was secured in 1690, the Orangemen's global mandate is "the defence of Protestant Christianity and the unity of the British Empire — one school, one flag, one language."

It is surprising enough that the good doctor would want to join such a society, let alone pull it off, but that he somehow contrived to infiltrate Court Dufferin No. 7 of the Independent Order of Foresters truly boggles the mind, the more so because the constitution of the IOF openly stated (as opposed to the unspoken, unwritten racist tenets adhered to by more "secret" societies) that membership was only available to "white Christian males."

There really is no extant wholly satisfactory explanation for Dr. Oronhyatekha acceptance in any of these organizations. At six foot three, 230 pounds, with luminous copper skin, a huge head, protruding eyes and memorable basso voice, Oronhyatekha could never have passed himself off as a white man, even had he wanted to.

The fact is Dr. O was inordinately proud of his native heritage. He never tried to hide it — the exact opposite. He wrote and published learned articles on the Mohawk language. He collected Indian artifacts from all over North America which he displayed prominently.

One thing is certain: Oronhyatekha was a beguiling, charismatic character and inveterate self-promoter. Setting up his first practice in Frankford, Ontario, he advertised his services as those of an Oxford physician who had trained with Dr. Acland in England.

Indeed, Dr. O had first met Dr. Acland when Dr. Acland accompanied the Prince of Wales on his trip to the Six Nations Reserve in 1860. What his advertisements failed to point out was the fact that Dr. Acland's degrees were in divinity rather than in Dr. O's alleged medical specialties, which the advertisements avowed were diseases of the throat and lungs as well as nervous disorders.

Regardless, since Frankford was near a large Mohawk reserve, Dr. O astutely added "Indian cures and herbal medicines" to his blurbs. He never looked back.

By 1870, three years after graduating from medical school, Dr. Oronhyatekha was well-enough positioned within the local medical establishment to be elected first secretary of the Hastings County Medical Association.

In 1871, he was invited to practise medicine in Stratford, Ontario with a Dr. Lucas. Politically active, his new partner enticed Dr. O into helping organize a local Conservative campaign. As a consequence, Oronhyatekha met Sir John A. Macdonald, Prime Minister of the newly minted Canada.

Like the Prince and his good offices on behalf of Oronhyatekha with Oxford University, Sir John was sufficiently impressed by Dr. O to recommend him for the job of consulting physician to the Mohawks at Tyendinaga Reserve near Ottawa, a patronage appointment with some prestige.

Perhaps momentarily overwhelmed by delusions of grandeur, Dr. O immediately overextended himself when he built a mansion to house his modest family in Napanee. Within less than a year, he was essentially bankrupt.

Moving to London, Ontario he opened a new practice and started over from scratch at the ripe old age of thirty-three.

Once again billing himself as an Oxford-educated physician and — with about the same amount of justification — a former government official, Dr. O began joining all of the fraternal, temperance and masonic organizations he could find in the area. One of them happened to be the Orange Society. The rest is history.

Whatever the reasons, however it happened, Dr. O took to the Independent Order of Foresters and their philosophy — which more than one observer has called "fraternal bunk" — like a duck to water.

He began a career of almost frantic, sometimes unsalaried, arguably fanatical activity with the IOF. His unbridled and seemingly sincere enthusiasm for the tenets of this particular kind of fraternalism were infectious. It was only a matter of months before he was High Chief Ranger of its Ontario High Court.

The Order was bankrupt — a schism had developed between the core American organization and the Canadian satellite — and all but 369 souls had jumped ship between 1878 and 1881, but Dr. O still travelled throughout the province at his own expense proselytizing fraternalism. In 1881, he was elected the first Supreme Chief Ranger of the Independent Order of Foresters, a position he held for the duration of his life.

Over the next decade, Dr. O single-handedly reconstituted the IOF as an international entity and a source of cradle-to-grave benefits for its members. In addition to life insurance, which was its schematic foundation, the Order had pension plans, weekly sick benefits, disability insurance and funeral coverage at prices with which traditional, old-line insurance companies could not compete.

Never one to shy away, Oronhyatekha proclaimed the IOF "the poor man's order."

Partly to allay public suspicion of the Order and partly to promote its products, Dr. O began to run full-page newspaper ads across the country detailing every aspect of the IOF's financial position and benefits, including its provision of up-to-the-minute "hourly sick pay-outs." He ran this campaign the way modern companies run their worldwide websites. The data was constantly changing, and was regularly updated, always to look better and better to the average citizen.

Oronhyatekha also had the sensibilities and sensitivities of the modern pollster. He seemed to be able to sense public opinion. In spite of the fact that the values of the IOF were arguably antithetical to his native heritage, Dr. O presented the IOF as a sound business operation run by sober, white, Christian men dedicated to the British Crown because that is what the majority of first-generation Scottish, Irish and English immigrants who populated the new country responded to.

The fact that he was a "Barnum let loose in the insurance business," as Dr. O was described in a 1951 *Maclean's* magazine article, does nothing to reconcile the contradictions inherent in what he did for a living and what he was.

By the time he died on August 6, 1907, the Independent Order of Foresters had become an international organization with more than a quarter of a million North American members and liquid assets in excess of eleven million dollars, making it the largest fraternal body on the continent.

The imprint of some of the more flamboyant characteristics of the IOF's Mohawk leader became bleached out by time and imperfect memory. For many years, it was regarded as a staid, stodgy, if somewhat secretive, insurance provider. However, in the 1990s, the family-values-oriented Order was rocked by a sex scandal involving none other than Dr. Oronhyatekha's 1990s counterpart, the Supreme Chief Ranger.

It seems the tall, lanky, high-living Texan executive had a penchant for certain things antithetical to Dr. O's devotion to high Anglicanism, monogamy and teetotalling. Nevertheless, evidently the Ranger from Texas shared with his predecessor a keen sense of the roll Barnums can play in the world of insurance.

When the wily, sexually active American agreed to resign in 1996 and take a multi-million-dollar golden parachute, the IOF had over 1,000 employees, over two million members, a solid balance sheet showing a $700-million-dollar cash surplus and assets of five billion dollars.

THE HEART OF THE MATTER

Montreal, 1890 — She was to all intents a fortunate orphan, raised by loving grandparents who provided a governess for her early education. A conventional child in many respects, she read *Little Women*, kept a diary full of her dreams and delighted in a Christmas stocking that included "a silver thimble, a black-handled tooth brush, half a dozen handkerchiefs." But by the time she was fifteen, Maude Abbott clearly had more on her mind than shopping for the contents of the first catalogue published by Timothy Eaton.

"Think of learning German, Latin and other languages in general," she wrote to herself in 1884. "Think of the loveliness of thinking that it entirely depended on myself whether I got on."

Applying herself to the process of "getting on" was not a problem for Maude Abbott. She had a boundless enthusiasm for learning, which would see her studying in Germany, Austria and Scotland before she settled into her life's work as a medical curator and a world authority on congenital heart ailments.

The Abbott surname belonged to Maude's grand-parents. Their daughter, Elizabeth, married the Reverend Jeremiah Babin but the marriage failed before Maude was even born. She was seven months old when her mother died of tuberculosis, leaving Maude and her sister, Alice, to be legally adopted by her grandparents.

Reverend William Abbott came to Canada in 1818 with his brother, Joseph, who was also an Anglican clergyman. They occupied charges in St. Andrews East and what is now known as Abbotsford, Quebec. Young Maude thrived in what she recalled as "the genial social atmosphere of old world culture and refinement" of her childhood. The Abbott family achieved prominence in the area, most notably through Maude's second cousin, John, the first Canadian-born Prime Minister in 1891.

But having relatives in high places was not going to help Maude realize her dream of attending McGill University. For years, McGill opposed "mixed classes" on moral grounds and claimed that separate sex class-es were not economically feasible.

A hero appeared in 1884 in the figure of Donald Smith (later Lord Strathcona) who endowed the university with a total of $120,000 specifically for the higher education of women. Two years later, Maude Abbott received a scholarship to enter the arts program, the only program McGill offered to female students.

When Grace Ritchie delivered the first valedictory address to McGill's "Donalda" students, she distinguished herself by challenging the university to expand its enlightened attitude by starting a medical course for women. She herself pursued medical studies at Kingston's Women's Medical College, which had opened its doors in 1883.

Around the time of Grace Ritchie's speech, Maude Abbott was beginning to consider what her options would be after graduation. The story goes that Maude sought her grandmother's counsel.

"May I be a doctor?" she asked.

"Dear child, you may be anything you like," Mrs. Abbott told her. What the progressive grandmother did not tell her eager charge was that McGill University would have to be pixillated by a lot of fairy dust and a World War before a woman would graduate from their medical school.

Maude started petitioning the faculty of medicine to open classes to women before she graduated in the arts. The idea was summarily rejected, even when Maude and her supporters raised $12,000 toward the expense.

One professor threatened to resign. Another despaired that while women might have some useful place in certain areas of medicine, they "would not have the nerve" in "difficult work" such as surgery.

He added: "And can you think of a patient in a critical case, waiting for half an hour while the medical lady fixes her bonnet or adjusts her bustle."

Although she considered anything less than a McGill education to be "inferior," Maude elected to attend Bishop's Medical College in Montreal. It was as close to McGill as she could get, since many McGill professors provided hospital instruction at Montreal General Hospital.

Access to hospital instruction was a critical issue to women attending medical college in those days. Grace Ritchie had paved the way for Maude at Bishop's. A knowledgeable, likable student, Ritchie impressed Bishop's staff when she spent a summer as a clinician at Montreal General Hospital, gaining a "ticket" permitting access to the wards. Bishop's lured Ritchie away from Kingston to spend her final year with them. She was a feather in their cap to wave at their McGill rivals.

What Montreal General had done for the amiable Ritchie began to have repercussions. Other women medical students from Kingston began applying for summer "tickets" to the teaching wards. Before graduating from Bishop's, Ritchie told Maude Abbott to send her twenty-dollar fee and her application right away.

Sure enough, the hospital started backtracking on entry for women, allegedly fearing an onslaught of ticket requests from women. Maude was caught in a "Catch-22" situation. On one hand, she had started classes at Bishop's without a hitch, but on the other she could not graduate without hospital experience. The hospital had taken her money but now they would not give her the ticket to teaching ward access that she had paid for.

She was contemplating a transfer to medical school in Philadelphia when her story hit the newspapers. At a delicate moment in Montreal General's annual fund-raising process, several of the largest subscribers refused to pay until Miss Abbott received her ticket. Her ticket arrived in the mail.

In 1894, Maude Abbott graduated with honours and accolades. It had been a lonely four years, in which she found herself decried by her peers as an aggressive "swot." Although shy by nature, apparently Maude would not hesitate to elbow her way to the front of any demonstration.   In keeping with her passion for being at the forefront, Maude embarked on postgraduate studies in Vienna, accompanied by her sister, Alice, who was pursuing music studies. She spent two years taking courses, including internal medicine and pathology, which were her special interests.

When the Abbott sisters returned to Montreal in 1897, Alice was recovering from a bout of diphtheria. A few years later, she suffered a nervous breakdown. Maude would care for her chronically invalid sister all her life.

To support the two of them, Dr. Abbott opened a practice for women and children. This drab follow-up to her European sojourn was brightened when two professors associated with McGill took an interest in clinical studies she had conducted in Vienna and assigned her to research projects. Although it was mandated that women could not present academic papers, Maude's statistical study on heart murmurs gained her recognition and unprecedented membership at the society where it was read. Another paper was delivered by a male colleague on her behalf to the Pathological Society in London, England, the first time research by a woman was recognized.

McGill finally began to see Dr. Abbott's scholarship and energy as a potential asset. In 1898, she was appointed as assistant curator of the university's medical museum. Since its beginnings in 1823, "specimens" had been accumulating in jars and bottles. Maude's task was to catalogue, classify and organize seventy-five years of pickled neglect.

On a tour of American museums, she met the Canadian physician who inspired her career as he did generations of medical practitioners. By then, William Osler was chief of medicine at Johns Hopkins Hospital in Baltimore. Dr. Osler shared Dr. Abbott's passion for pathology, and he was responsible for a good many of the specimens at McGill which she would be maintaining. He told her that the museum was a great opportunity and one that would provide a valuable teaching tool. "He gently dropped a seed that dominated all my future work," said Maude.

In 1905, Osler was compiling the book *System of Medicine* and he asked Maude to contribute on the topic of congenital heart disease. The monograph she submitted included a statistical analysis of more than 400 cases. Osler declared it "far and away the best thing ever written on the subject" and Abbott became known internationally as an authority. A dozen years before the first female doctors would graduate from McGill in 1922, the university granted Maude an honorary degree M.D., C.M. (*honoris causa*), and she began lecturing in pathology.

The museum also flourished. Students enjoyed stopping by and asking questions. Maude formed associations with other medical museums, as well as cataloguing the Canadian Army Medical Museum. She also served as editor of the *Canadian Medical Association Journal*, wrote a definitive history of medicine in Quebec and chaired the Federation of Medical Women of Canada.

It has been said that McGill University never quite appreciated the whirlwind wunderkind that it had in the woman who was often called "Maudie." Her desk was a chaos of papers. Sometimes she set such a dizzying schedule for herself that she forgot to eat. Notebooks had a habit of slipping from her fingers, and train tickets found ways of escaping her. She was consumed by her work, as evidenced by a formalin stain from one of her beloved samples that ended up on an evening gown.

Although she received offers of full professorships from other universities, Dr. Abbott strayed from McGill only once in the mid-1920s when Women's Medical College in Pennsylvannia lured her away at double her salary. When she returned to McGill, she was made an assistant professor, a designation that lasted until her reluctant retirement in 1936.

At sixty-seven, Dr. Abbott embarked on a lecture tour, which coincided with the publication of her classic work *Atlas of Congenital Heart Disease*. Always prone to accidents, she was sixty-nine when she was crushed between two streetcars in Montreal. Recovering in the hospital, she surrounded herself with books and papers. The following year she received a Carnegie grant to write a textbook, but she suffered a cerebral hemorrhage and died in September, 1940, before its completion.

"Work is fundamental to the onward march of science," Maude Abbott said in the valedictory address she delivered to her graduating class in 1890, "It is at the bottom of every great and good action that was ever done; it underlies the formation of all true character."

A scholar, a teacher and a curator, she was hailed as "a living force in the medicine of her generation." Ultimately, the "loveliness" of depending on herself to "get on" that Maude dreamed of as a child became her reality.

H₂O + MYSTERIOUS GREY POWDER = SUNSHINE + \$\$\$\$

Saguenay Valley, Quebec, 1892 — Turn-of-the-century industrial revolutionary Thomas Leopold Willson was one of those visionaries who could not see the forest for the opportunity. He earned several fortunes and gambled them all on the potential he saw in the uncompromising wilderness of the Saguenay River Valley.

Willson's passion was not wilderness for wilderness's sake. He saw the future in the dark recesses of that forest. To him, the raging Saguenay River represented an inexhaustible source of hydro-electric power. By 1908, Willson had acquired vast land, timber and water rights in the valley, encompassing tens of thousands of acres. As usual, he had big, big plans.

No slick grifter, Willson was a chronic and hugely successful inventor. In Canada alone, he held more than sixty patents. If even half of the proceeds had been properly managed, the return would have provided for a dozen dynasties. Willson managed to keep most of his millions and his dreams, until he met American tobacco and textile tycoon James Buchanan Duke.

Young Thomas "Leo" came from a prominent family. His grandfather was the Honourable John Willson, a member of the Legislative Assembly of Upper Canada who was known as "the Father of the Common Schools Act." One of nine children, his father (also named Thomas) became a minister, but he always had a few irons in the entrepreneurial fire, which caused his downfall. He died when his eldest son was fourteen after losing everything due to a loan guarantee that went bad and a failed attempt at manufacturing.

Forced to move from the family farm in Princeton, Ontario, the family settled in Hamilton. The widow Rachel Sabina Willson, a character in her own right, supported her two sons by taking in lodgers, teaching painting and giving lessons on the Spanish guitar.

A precocious youngster, Willson built a steam-driven generator and an experimental arc light system in the upstairs loft over a blacksmith's shop. In those days, electricity was not taken for granted. It was regarded as magical rather than scientific. Willson's arc lights attracted so much attention they had to be moved from the smithy's to Dundurn Park to accommodate the curious hordes. Forging a role for himself, the blacksmith became a business partner, taking orders for the lighting system from businesses and towns far and wide.

In the early days of electricity the big problem was the production of steady, even power, a problem that Willson had not solved. His arc lights were forever flickering and blinking on and off. Enthusiasm for them waned, transforming the buoyant business partners into bankrupts.

The faded local hero went to New York City where he worked at jobs involving electricity and smelting. He also acquired business skills and developed a new interest — aluminum.

In 1891, aluminum was a new metal and astonishingly expensive to produce. Willson was convinced that there had to be a cheaper means of production. He needed cash and a steady source of power, sufficient to fire a blast furnace. Finding both in Major James Morehead, a wealthy mill owner from North Carolina, the Willson Aluminum Company was formed in Spray, N.C.

The way Willson talked about the process it had more in common with medieval alchemy than modern science. He even speculated about how his "New Science" could be applied to produce commercial diamonds. Many months later, Willson's talk was wearing thin and his experiments yielded nothing but frustration. He was unaware that others in the field had already just discovered a much better, less expensive way to produce aluminum in France.

The Major's patience and money had just about run out when Willson stumbled on the thing that was going to change both their lives forever.

On May 2, 1892, Willson directed his assistants to mix a specific amount of coal, lime and tar then heat the mixture in the blast furnace to 5,500 degrees centigrade.

The average person might not have seen anything revelatory in the fact that a lump of grey, turgid dirt heated to 5,500 degrees caused a violent reaction when dropped into a bucket of cold water, but Thomas Willson was not the average person.

At the heart of science is repetition. The next time he did it, Willson put an oil-soaked rag on the end of a long pole, and, just for the heck of it, lit it on fire and held it over the water in which the heated lump of dirt had been dropped.

A flame leapt between the rag and the broiling water. When he pulled the rag away, the flame disappeared. Willson knew he had discovered something but had no idea what.

In Thomas Willson were combined two normally apostate talents. Not only was he capable of recognizing a discovery when he made one, he was amazingly adroit at realizing its commercial potential.

He knew instinctively that a gas that burns almost always has commercial value. A gas produced by dumping cheap lumps of heated dirt in plain water might have unlimited commercial potential.

Willson sent a description of his process and sample of his "unique" mixture of coal, lime and tar to the distinguished scientist William Thomson at the University of Glasgow. The response was a perfunctory "nothing new" note. Heated calcium carbide always produces bubbles of highly volatile acetylene gas in water, the professor wrote.

What was new was the actual accident of the discovery. Willson's method of producing both the carbide and the gas was tens of thousands of times cheaper than any previously discovered method.

Kerosene had virtually led the world out of the dark ages when it replaced candlelight in the 1850s. Compared to candles, the light kerosene provided was startlingly bright. The light acetylene produced was like sunlight, containing every colour in the spectrum. By the light of acetylene it was possible to grow plants. The possibilities seemed endless.

Willson's formula: Hot dirt + water = artificial sunlight + $$$.

In 1895, "Carbide" Willson sold his American patents to the newly formed Union Carbide company and the rest is, as they say, industrial history.

Willson got married and returned to Canada with ample funds to establish an all-Canadian carbide works at Merriton, near St. Catharines, Ontario on the Niagara Peninsula. The new facility included the first hydro-electric plant built in Canada and the largest on the North American continent.

Those were prosperous years for Willson. He moved his family to Woodstock, Ontario and formed a partnership with a local businessman named James Sutherland, who became a minister in Sir Wilfrid Laurier's cabinet.

Sutherland convinced Willson to move to Ottawa. In 1904, Willson established two more plants, one on Victoria Island in the Ottawa River and the other in Shawinigan, Quebec. Still, he could not keep up with demand.

By the time electricity made acetylene-fuelled light obsolete, Willson had adapted and made another fortune with oxy-acetylene torches. It had just been discovered that oxygen combined with acetylene would produce a flame that would cut through steel, a technology that revolutionized industry in North America.

While his wealth continued to grow exponentially, Willson grew restless. He had already started acquiring water and timber rights in the Saguenay Valley when he was temporarily distracted by an incident in Kingston, Ontario.

Marine buoys were illuminated by acetylene but in such a way that the buoys had to be refuelled. A beacon blew while being refilled at the Kingston docks, killing four people.

A few months later Willson filed the patents on a new type of navigational marker, it effectively functioned as a mini-carbide-acetylene factory. Willson's markers generated their own light and never had to be refilled. By 1906, his Marine Signal Company was filling orders from over forty countries. Willson made another fortune.

Willson's carbide seemed to transform everything he touched into gold. It turned out that calcium carbide could "fix" or capture nitrogen, thereby making it possible to store the gas as a solid.

Suddenly it dawned on Willson that his factories that already produced tons of calcium carbide and acetylene every day could also be used to produce a nitrogenous fertilizer.

Artificial or manmade fertilizers were already seen as elixirs of life. But they were derived from the Chilean guano fields where bird droppings were scraped from the rocks and shipped around the tip of South America. By the turn of the century, the guano fields were virtually exhausted.

The so-called superphosphates interested Willson. Soon he had perfected the manufacturing process, producing the most powerful fertilizer on the planet.

Willson was living at Meech Lake, where he was as restless and dissatisfied as his California-born wife, Mary, was calm and contented. All Willson saw when he looked out his window on the magnificent landscape was a source of unlimited power. A lake the size of Meech high in the Gatineau Hills had to have an outlet somewhere. Wherever that was, the water could be easily be channelled.

He was thinking about the future and the Saguenay Valley and hydro-electric power. Wealthy beyond words, bored and frustrated, he began to sell off his holdings to finance further acquisitions in the Saguenay Valley. In 1909, a Buffalo, N.Y. firm bought the Marine Signal Company. He divested himself of his carbide plants. He even sold his Canadian patents.

In 1911, he damned the small river below Meech Lake and built a private hydro-electric station hidden in the woods and a factory for the production of his superphosphate agricultural supplements. He saw in his private Meech Lake project the microcosm of his plans for the Saguenay River Valley. But it would cost more money than even Willson had stockpiled. He was in the process of mortgaging everything he owned when he met James Buchanan Duke.

Willson chartered a private train to take the fabulously wealthy Duke into the Saguenay wilderness, to show him — with style and flair — where the real future lay.

Duke agreed to lend the necessary $1.5 million, but in return he wanted as security the only thing Willson had left — the Saguenay properties. Willson foolishly agreed. A year later, the plant was up and running, but Willson found himself cash-strapped. He missed one interest payment and the wilderness belonged to Duke.

Willson was down but not out. Although he had sold his companies and his Canadian patents, there was always Newfoundland, as yet an independent colony. (Newfoundland did not join Canada until 1949.) He was able to build yet another carbide factory with impunity on the Rock, starting again from ground zero. By July, 1914, he had guarantees of over $10 million from British investors. Then the outbreak of the First World War cut off all foreign capital investments.

Thomas "Carbide" Willson was in New York four days before Christmas in 1915 hustling new sources of funding when he had a heart attack and died alone in a hotel room. He was forty-five.

James Buchanan Duke sold Willson's timber and water rights to the American industrialist Arthur Vining Davis, who established the vast aluminum industry that made the Saguenay area world-famous.

When Duke died he left his fortune, as vast as the Saguenay River Valley wilderness, to his ten-year-old daughter Doris. Until she disappeared five decades later, Ms. Duke was the richest woman in the world.

RUST NEVER SLEEPS

Prairies, 1916 — The language of the plant disease known as "rust" is an ugly piece of botanical business. In ideal circumstances, when the weather is warm and moist at least one-third of the day, yellow, orange or reddish "pustules" form in raised ovals on the stems, heads or leaves of the wheat plant. Each pustule may contain as many as 1,000 "urediospores," that attach themselves as reddish-brown powder to clothing or machinery that brushes them. They can move with the wind, like a "slinking demon," until healthy plants wither and seed development is arrested. What survives is a low grade of grain, or nothing more than straw.

Production in the Canadian wheat industry soared from 63 million bushels in 1901 to 300 million bushels in 1911. The development of Marquis wheat by Dominion Cerealist Charles Saunders expanded the harvest season and earned international acclaim for

Western farmers. The first harvest after Canada's entry into World War I yielded a bumper crop of 360 million bushels, despite a dry spring and a diminished farm labour force.

Disaster in the form of stem rust (*Puccinia graminis*) struck with a vengeance in 1916. Losses approached $200 million and the effect of the infection cast a pall on the future of Western wheat. Previous attempts at scouring the scourge by burning straw piles and field stubble had proved useless. The spores were airborne, blown north from Mexico and the southern United States. Then they waited for weather conditions to favour their development to epidemic proportions that spelled disaster. No amount of burning or tilling could stop the wind.

Scientists scrambled to find a solution. Conferences were organized, enjoining the talents of the National Research Council, the federal Department of Agriculture and leading plant botanists and biologists at three universities.

Margaret Newton was attending McGill University in 1917. She specialized in botany at Macdonald College, where she earned the distinction of being one of the first female students to graduate from an agricultural college, which she did with honours, including a Governor General's gold medal.

When one of her professors was called away to offer his advice about the problem of rust, Margaret was asked to maintain his ongoing experiments. In the process, she conducted her own experiments and discovered a vital clue.

Rust truly did not sleep. When ten spores where applied to ten identical wheat specimens, Newton found that the results were different. Instead of one organism, rust had many "races."

Scientists had imagined that they could control the disease by developing a single strain of wheat capable of resisting the disease. Dr. W.P. Thompson at the University of Saskatchewan had already proposed the notion of manipulating plant genetics to combine strains of wheat that showed resistance to rust with popular and profitable strains of wheat such as Marquis. However, Margaret Newton had isolated and identified at least fourteen races of rust and she warned that even more could result from mutation and hybridization. The battle against rust was going to be more complex than anyone had imagined, and the young woman from McGill would devote a lifetime of study to unravelling its mysteries. In the end, it would be rust that ruined her health.

There were five children in the Newton family — three boys and two girls. Their father, John, was a chemist, and they grew up on a farm near the western Quebec town of Plaisance. Education was a family priority. Each and every one of the Newton children graduated from McGill university and each and every one of them went on to earn PhDs.

After Margaret received her doctorate at the University of Minnesota, she continued her research as a professor of plant pathology at the University of Saskatchewan.

Margaret Newton was thirty-eight when she joined the Associate Committee on Cereal Rust at the newly constructed Dominion Rust Research Laboratory that opened on the grounds of the University of Manitoba in 1925. The goal of the "Rust Lab" was to create "custom made" strains of wheat that could resist disease while retaining the bread-making qualities that Canadian wheat was famous for. As a result, new varieties such as Renown, Apex, Regent, Redman and Thatcher and Selkirk were developed by Canadian and American scientists and plant breeders.

In her career Dr. Newton isolated approximately 150 different strains of rust. She wrote forty-two scientific papers and became an international authority, lecturing around the world.

When she visited the Plant Breeding Institute at Leningrad in 1933, the Russian government wanted her to carry out research and studies on the origins of rust, which was thought to be in Turkestan. She was offered ample funding, a team of fifty scientists, even a fleet of camels for desert travel.

Margaret is said to have been tempted to accept, until her brother, Robert, who had become the Dean of Agriculture and the President of the University of Alberta, advised her that: "The overseas assignment could be a rich experience but the work in rust research in Canada would suffer." She stayed.

All of the years of working with spores took their toll. In 1945, Newton was forced to retire because of lung problems that produced a chronic asthmatic condition. When the Canadian government balked at paying her full pension, Western farmers mounted a petition in protest noting that: "This woman has saved the country millions of dollars." They were successful.

In 1948, Margaret Newton became the first woman to receive the Flavelle Medal of the Royal Society of Canada for her outstanding contribution to biological science, an award that was first presented to Sir Charles Saunders, the "father" of Canadian wheat.

FEETS DON'T FAIL ME NOW

Williamsburg, Ontario, 1932 — Between 1932 and 1942, millions of people from all over the world made a pilgrimage to a tiny Ontario village between Cornwall and Gananoque.

Princes from as far away as India, paupers who rode the rails, society matrons, Hollywood moguls such as Louis B. Mayer, British nobility, even the American president's wife, Eleanor Roosevelt — tens of thousands of people, day-in and day-out, found their way to Williamsburg, Ontario to put their feet in the hands of Dr. Mahlon W. Locke.

According to the tabloids of the day Dr. Locke could virtually raise the dead. He was the Canadian "miracle man" with "x-ray hands."

On the other hand the medical profession dismissed him as "a quack."

But Dr. Mahlon W. Locke was no quack.

A fully qualified medical doctor, he held the prestigious triple licentiate from the Royal College of

Surgeons, Edinburgh, the Royal College of Physicians, Edinburgh and the Royal Faculty of Physicians and Surgeons, Glasgow.

Born on a farm at Dixon's Corners, seven miles west of Williamsburg, on Valentine's Day, 1880, Mahlon Locke showed an early aptitude for agriculture. This was a good thing because his father died suddenly in 1888 and eight-year-old Mahlon had to take on responsibility for the farm and the family including his mother and two younger brothers.

Because he was good with animals, Mahlon reasoned that he might be good with people and decided to go into medicine. He finally entered the medical program at Queen's University at the age of twenty-one. An exceptional student, he graduated four years later and returned to Dixon's Corners to set up practice with his new stepfather, Dr. G.W. Collison.

With only fifteen dollars to show for six months' work, a discouraged young Dr. Locke jumped at the chance to work at Algoma Steel in Sudbury for a guaranteed $100 a month.

The following year he was accepted in a postgraduate program at the Royal Infirmary in Edinburgh, Scotland where, among many other things, he learned the difficult techniques of foot manipulation and developed his theory of good health.

"Nobody can feel well if his feet are sick," he said. "I put my patients' feet right and Nature does the healing."

To put it simply, Dr. Locke theorized that manipulating the arches relieved pressure on the large nerve
which ended in the foot. Increased healthy blood circulation in that area would, in turn, help rid the blood-
stream of impurities.

In 1908, he returned to Williamsburg and began to
practise the kind of medicine for which the modern
age has become increasingly nostalgic. He made
horse-and-buggy house calls — midday and midnight
runs to deliver babies, set broken bones or stitch up
split heads.

Early on, Dr. Locke observed that too many of the
locals suffered from flat feet and rheumatism for the
co-existence of the two conditions to be purely coinci-
dental.

For instance, a local blacksmith named Peter
Beckstead whom Dr. Locke began treating in 1908 had
been as strong as the horses he shod until crippling
joint pain made it virtually impossible for him to work.

To the blacksmith's amazement, Dr. Locke began
fiddling with his feet, pressing his arches, spreading
and pulling his toes. The blacksmith was even more
surprised when the debilitating pain began to subside
after half a dozen treatments.

Dr. Locke then took Mr. Beckstead to the local
shoemaker and had the cobbler fit the smith's shoes
with leather inserts. The doctor called the inserts
"cookies." He said the cookies would keep the blacksmith's arches in place and strengthen his foot muscles.

Fully recovered, Peter Beckstead kept shoeing horses until the day he died twenty-five years later.

Dr. Locke practised his unique brand of foot-oriented medicine in relative obscurity for two decades. Because he consistently got good results, and because the locals found having their feet played with somewhat unusual, his reputation spread slowly by word-of-mouth beyond the township.

From Williamsburg to the town of Morrisburg on the shores of the St. Lawrence River is a mere six miles. From Morrisburg it is a short ferry ride to New York State.

In 1928, Frank Coughlin, an arthritic newspaperman from Lockport, New York was referred to the Williamsburg clinic by an elderly Catholic priest who suffered from the same disorder until he put his feet in Dr. Locke's hands. Coughlin's condition had been deemed so serious that he was scheduled for potentially dangerous surgery. After Locke's foot manipulation treatment, the reporter cancelled his surgery and wrote a glowing report that was reprinted in dozens of American newspapers.

By 1930, Dr. Locke was seeing up to 300 people a day. His reputation spread like a grass fire. By the summer of 1931, the number had swelled to almost 1,000.

That summer Dr. Locke met the American writer Rex Beach. Beach had penned a dozen popular biographies, a couple of successful adventure novels and the screenplay for *The Spoilers*, a 1914 silent picture about the gold rush.

While on a golfing holiday in Ottawa, Beach kept complaining about his fallen arches. One of his companions jokingly suggested that if he was that badly hobbled, he should probably visit the famous foot doctor in nearby Williamsburg.

What Rex Beach witnessed and experienced led him to write a feature article in *Cosmopolitan* magazine, which appeared in August, 1932. After that, Dr. Locke never had another moment to himself.

The road from Ottawa to Williamsburg had been a potholed, gravel cart track, when Beach made his first visit. Three years later, he returned to find it transformed into a paved two-lane highway congested with cars, buses and trucks. Many were hung with signs such as "To Williamsburg and Dr. Locke," and "Dr. Locke or Bust."

The closer Beach got to the centre of Williamsburg (which boasted a population of a few less than 300) the slower traffic became until it virtually stood still.

People in wheelchairs rolled along the roadside. It was not uncommon to see a person on a stretcher being wheeled through the streets. Every second pedestrian seemed to be on crutches.

Two ferries were crossing from Waddington, New York to Morrisburg every quarter of an hour from 7 a.m. until midnight, seven days a week, instead of one every hour, eight hours a day, five days a week as had been the service before Dr. Locke's foot manipulation therapy seized the popular imagination. Transcontinental trains were making regular, unprecedented stops at Morrisburg.

Two hotels, one with 125 rooms, were built and constantly full. The *Rapids Queen*, an ocean liner with sixty-five staterooms and a ballroom, was permanently anchored at Morrisburg to accommodate the overflow. Instead of three struggling restaurants, twenty-three now thrived.

While the rest of the country strangled in the grip of the worst depression in the history of North America, the townsfolk of Williamsburg and Morrisburg were literally run off their feet servicing the patrons of the foot doctor.

Rex Beach found Dr. Locke where he was most every day for the last fifteen years of his life, surrounded by a circus-throng of humanity, feeling feet on the lawn beside his house.

Dr. Locke sat at the hub of "The Circle" — a series of fourteen iron pipes that surrounded his swivel chair like giant spokes. The pipes marked runways down which patients moved on camp stools until they reached the wooden chairs arranged in a circle around Dr. Locke.

After years of trampling, the west lawn of his house had been covered with concrete. Elderly patients pooled resources and built a wooden pavilion to shelter the hundreds upon hundreds of afflicted and infirm who waited patiently for the doctor's attention.

In his early fifties, Dr. Locke radiated strength. He was a large man with a massive head, penetrating blue eyes and thick shoulders. A little ruffled and unkempt, he worked in shirt sleeves, without a collar or tie. His diagnoses were based only on what he saw and felt in front of him. Grasping each stockinged foot, he would press up on the arch with one quick movement of his thumb while he twisted the toes down and out with the other hand. At the end of each day, he painted his aching thumbs with iodine.

Although a man of few words, Locke had a sense of humour and laughed easily. When a patient complaining of shoulder pain asked him why she had to take her shoes off for treatment he responded with a question: "When you step on a dog's tail, which end yelps?"

He had no time for pretence. He treated everyone, rich or poor, on a first-come, first-served basis. Each consultation cost a dollar. There is an apocryphal story about a well-dressed woman who pushed her way to the front of one of the lines, proclaiming herself "a millionaire." To which Dr. Locke is alleged to have replied, "Madam, so am I. Get back in line."

With the occasional stop to unwind his chair, or go into the house and empty his pockets of dollar bills, Dr. Locke sprang from patient to patient with lightning speed, probing and manipulating as many as ten feet a minute.

During the Dirty Thirties, millions of words were written about Dr. Locke. There were thousands of newspaper columns, hundreds of magazine articles, several biographies and even a novel.

He repeatedly said he cared nothing for money, while capriciously noting that he was probably the only man in the world who had literally made a million dollars with his own two hands. At the height of his fame, he was manipulating as many as 2,700 people's feet twice a day, seven days a week. At ten dollars a pair, 9,000 pairs of Dr. Locke's arch-support–enhanced shoes walked out of Williamsburg before he sold the patent for $30,000.

In spite of glowing testimonials from grateful patients, among them a number of his colleagues, the medical establishment stubbornly maintained that Dr. Locke's healing ways could be explained away by mass hysteria and hypnosis.

"I don't give a damn," was Dr. Locke's response. "A great many [of my patients] have been to the foremost specialists and the best hospitals both here and abroad and have been pronounced incurable."

Rex Beach wrote: "This is no mere laying on of hands: there are no instantaneous cures, no miracles. He [Dr. Locke] has a peculiar knowledge and an uncanny skill: improvement is gradual and sure."

Locke turned down an offer from the prestigious Mayo Clinic in Rochester, N.Y. He said he didn't want to work "like a mule in the back room" when he could run his own show in Williamsburg. Well-respected in the community, he declined offers to enter politics.

Although he worked year-round, with no time off except a week at Christmas, Locke found time for a hobby in farming, which grew to include seventeen properties. One of his Holstein cows set a world record for milk and butter production.

Despite the fact that he gave demonstrations and opened his clinic to examination by other physicians, Mahlon Locke was never fully able to translate the secret of his "manipulative surgery." He suffered a fatal stroke one week shy of his seventy-first birthday, after trying to push his 1942 Cadillac out of a snow-filled ditch.

IS IT A BIRD? IS IT A PLANE? NO, IT'S AN ARROW!

Ottawa, 1959 — Few Canadian stories transcend the details of their history and become part of the national consciousness, but that's what happened when Prime Minister John Diefenbaker cancelled the Avro Arrow C 150 project on February 20, 1959. Faster than Diefenbaker's fulmination, the Arrow disappeared into myth.

Eleven months before the cancellation, thousands of employees of A.V. Roe Canada Limited had cheered the thirty-five-minute maiden flight of the advanced supersonic twin-engine, all-weather interceptor jet aircraft.

When Diefenbaker made his announcement to a hushed House of Commons, those same employees immediately lost their jobs and their collective dream to fulfil what Minister of National Defence George Pearkes had eighteen months earlier hailed as "a new era for Canada in the air."

Four decades later, controversy and intrigue continues to surround this amazing airplane. The fact that everything to do with the Arrow including all existing planes, components, tooling, drawings and documentation were ordered destroyed certainly contributed to its mystique.

There is even a persistent rumour that one Arrow was surreptitiously saved and remains hidden away to this day.

To date, there have been six non-fiction books, two books of fiction, a play, dozens upon dozens of articles and a mini-series aired on national television about the Avro Arrow and its fate. There is an Arrow fan club and a rather elaborate and well-developed website.

Canada has a tradition of making serious contributions to advances in aviation — from W.R. Turnbull's perfection of the electrically operated variable-pitch propeller in 1927 to the Spar Aerospace Canadarm. The Avro Arrow was an exceptional example in this distinguished history.

A.V. Roe Canada, although set up by a British company, was always fully financed in Canada. After World War II, the Canadian military, with tutelage from their American cousins, supposed that the major postwar threat to the North American continent was long-range, high-altitude bombers flying over the Arctic.

What was needed was a unique, new aircraft to protect this difficult frontier. It was decided that the best approach would be to design and build it in Canada.

The CF 100, Canada's "home-designed and built front-line fighter plane" was the precursor to the Avro CF 150 Arrow. Six hundred and ninety-two CF 100s were built and successfully put into service all over the world.

In the early 1950s, the Canadian government decided to follow the same course to replace the CF 100s. Military strategists predicted that the Cold War threat to the North American continent would evolve into supersonic, Soviet bombers. A new plane would need to be ready for service in the early 1960s. But the specifications seemed to be out of a science fiction novel.

The new aircraft had to be able to cruise and fight at Mach 1.5 (one-and-a-half times the speed of sound), at an altitude of 50,000 feet (very high) and be capable of pulling 2g in manoeuvres with no loss of speed or altitude (2g in a manoeuvre means that the pilot's weight on the seat is twice that of level flight, twice the pull of gravity).

The aircraft was to have a range of at least 200 nautical miles and be capable of reaching maximum speed and altitude in less than five minutes from the time its engine was started.

No one else in the world had been able to build an aircraft that would even come close to fulfilling such stringent demands.

With its all-Canadian designed and built Iroquois engine, the Arrow exceeded the specifications. A number of innovations were tossed in for good measure. For instance, the design of a removable armament pack aerodynamically integrated with the aircraft meant that whatever was carried in the pack had no effect on the airplane's speed or manoeuvrability.

The Arrow was conceived to be the delivery component of a rather elaborate, high-tech system of defence. That system included an airplane, airborne fire control systems, weapons and a ground-based radar communications system.

The designers of the Arrow worked feverishly to build actual aircraft, testing each design and alteration with elaborate computer models and simulations. Meanwhile, their political masters fiddled and fudged.

Originally, they were to pick up the fire control system from the Americans; then they were directed to switch to a Canadian-designed system called Astra. Then it was switched back to Hughes. The choice of weapons went back and forth, at the behest of the RCAF and the government, from American to Canadian to American-made missiles. The ground-based radar system became part of the Canadian/ American North American Air Defence Command (NORAD) set up in 1957.

The Arrow was nothing if not adaptable. Missiles such as the American Falcon, the Canadian Velvet Glove or modified Sparrow were debated and substituted one for the other without any noticeable effect on the aircraft's performance and manoeuvrability. During one test flight, the Arrow reached a speed of Mach 1.96, even though the plane was powered by an inferior American-built engine.

Then it was gone. There was no Parliamentary debate, no public discussion. The decision was made by Diefenbaker and a few members of his Cabinet in secret, behind closed doors. Diefenbaker simply announced the end of the Avro Arrow in Parliament on February 20, 1959 and that was that. Crawford Gordon, President and General Manager of A.V. Roe, announced the cancellation over the plant public-address system. With it came a notice of termination. That very day, A.V. Roe laid off 14,000 workers. Six prototypes went to the chopping block.

Nagging, unanswered questions still surround the Arrow. For instance, why did the government and the minister responsible lie about their immediate and inexplicable plans to destroy every Arrow prototype and everything having anything to do with the project?

The Honourable Raymond O'Hurley, then Minister of Defence Production in the Diefenbaker government, started out at first assuring the press that no order had been given to destroy the Arrow.

When caught out in that lie, he simply gave them another. He said such action was routine with classified projects; he had been mistaken in the first instance and his office had not actually been consulted. Recent revelations show exactly the opposite to have been true. A memo dated March 4, 1959 from O'Hurley's office shows he was delivering the orders for the total eradication of the Arrow.

Was the scrapping of the Arrow project in part a political payoff for favours curried from Duplessis and his Quebec liberal government?

Why was BOMARC, the American ground-to-air missile system, blithely accepted by the Canadian government as a substitute for the Arrow when BOMARC's failure was imminent and predictable?

Who initiated the Defence Production Sharing Agreement with the U.S. and why?

Why was the national media often ill-disposed to the Arrow project? Diefenbaker and his Cabinet wrongly interpreted the negative reportage as a reflection of public opinion that supported what they had wanted to do since as early as 1957.

Why was there no attempt to maintain and profit from technology transfers and spin-offs that were legion with a high-technology project as diverse and successful as the Avro Arrow?

Some commentators see in the Avro Arrow and its fate a turning point where Canada once and for all relinquished control over its own destiny and ceded to a diminutive garrison mentality and perpetual branch-plant economy.

Whereas these questions and the many others will continue to be asked by historians and students of the

Diefenbaker era and the Avro Arrow, the plane itself will always exist as a perfect machine in a special place beyond sound and light.

CREATIVITY
&
ACTIVITY

THE WISE CHILD

PORTRAIT OF THE ARTIST AS YOUNG WOMEN

A GENTLEMAN AND A SCULLER

THE BATTLE OF THE BLOOMERS

THE COWBOY FROM QUEBEC

A MAN IN A HURRY

SPONTANEOUS COMBUSTION

MORE STARS THAN HEAVEN

THE WISE CHILD

Halifax, Nova Scotia, 1835 — If history conveys any truth, at least one axiom is that Canadians make inordinately Good Neighbours. Generous to a fault, we have, willy nilly, given our American cousins basketball, baseball, even the comic book hero Superman. Likewise, our sayings and clichés have crossed the 49th parallel as easily as a Canadian comedian with a Green Card, destined to be adopted by that larger popular culture as their own.

However, when it is "raining cats and dogs" or if something happens "quick as wink," the description is purely Canadian.

Expressions and maxims, ranging from the proverbial "Jack of all trades and master of none," to the pragmatic "an ounce of prevention is worth a pound of cure," were the creations of nineteeth-century Nova Scotia judge, historian and humourist Thomas Chandler Haliburton. Americans may use the terms as freely as Canadians, but if they wish to claim them as homegrown, they are (as Haliburton would have it) "barking up the wrong tree."

A prodigious snob given to proselytizing and pontificating about the Old World and beloved England, Haliburton decided early on that the only way to reach his lazy, ignorant fellow colonists, was to employ humour "to render subjects attractive that in themselves are generally considered as too dry and deep for general reading." The son of Loyalists, he despised Americans on one hand, but also admired their industriousness and economic expansion.

American republicans called Nova Scotia "Nova Scarcity," but Haliburton was convinced that in consideration of the abundant resources of the province, a transportation initiative to improve the flow of goods and a modicum of enterprise from the citizenry could transform the region to the level of prosperity it deserved.

The vehicle for Haliburton's moral, political rails against hypocrisy and sloth was a character named Sam Slick, a wayfaring Odysseus in the guise of a Yankee clockmaker. As a travelling salesman and a con man, Sam Slick's mission was to sell clocks that cost him $6.50 to the great unwashed for $40 and in the process reveal the frailties of "human natur" and "some pretty home truths."

A cacaphony of ungrammatical colloquialisms characterize Haliburton's Slick character, who oils his "marks" with "soft sawdur" before closing a deal. As

Dr. Watson did for Sherlock Holmes, a Squire named Tom Poker served as the narrator in Haliburton's episodic, often plotless stories that were tantamount to an opinionated lay sermon.

"I reckon they are bad off for inns in this country," the Squire reports Sam Slick saying. "When a feller is too lazy to work here, he paints his name over his door and calls it a tavern, and as likes as not he makes the whole neighbourhood as lazy as himself."

Haliburton's Sam Slick stories were first published by his good friend Joseph Howe in Howe's liberal newspaper *The Novascotian* in 1835 under the heading "Recollections of Nova Scotia." After the first twenty-two installments, requests for reprints spurred Howe to publish the collected stories as *The Clockmaker; or the Sayings and Doings of Sam Slick, of Slickville*. More than seventy editions of the book were published in Canada, the United States and Britain, making Haliburton the first Canadian writer to gain an international reputation.

Thomas Chandler Haliburton was forty years old when *The Clockmaker* was published. Like his father and his father before him, he was a Tory and a lawyer. Elected to the Nova Scotia House of Assembly in 1826, he proceeded to write bills and make a name for himself as a formidable orator. When the council disallowed one of his bills, Haliburton lambasted them, creating a memorable description of senators that resonates to this day.

Calling the members, all of whom in their time were men of prominence, "twelve dignified, deep read, pensioned, old ladies . . . filled with prejudices and whims like all other antiquated spinsters," he declared that he himself had no time for "petticoat government."

After three years, Haliburton found himself disenchanted with politics. The death of his father left a judgeship opening in Nova Scotia's Inferior Court of Common Pleas and T.C. filled it. He had already written two scholarly works, *A General Description of Nova Scotia* (1823), which was published anonymously, and an ambitious two-volume work, *An Historical and Statistical Account of Nova Scotia*, which received critical acclaim but left its publisher, Joseph Howe, with a heavy burden of debt.

By the time Howe published *The Clockmaker* in 1936, the variance of political opinions between the two friends had become pronounced. Judge Haliburton had urged a jury to convict Howe on a charge of libel that had been brought against him after he published a letter accusing officials of corruption. Howe defended himself in a six-hour oratory that included a description of local magistrates as "the most negligent and imbecile . . . that ever mismanaged a people's affairs." Howe won the case and his popularity soared.

Despite the strain on the friendship, Howe and Haliburton travelled to England together in 1938 for what was called "the grand tour." Howe returned to Nova Scotia to champion the cause of reform and advocate responsible government. Haliburton extended his stay in England, where he enjoyed considerable fame and success, often at the expense of Howe, whose thinly disguised exploits became the target of some of Haliburton's most pointed satire in *The Attaché; or, Sam Slick in England*.

While Howe advocated a separation of church and state, Haliburton advocated a strengthening, believing that the colony would benefit from more government by Britain rather than less. The rupture in the friendship was further scarred when Haliburton reneged on a busines deal. The two men even participated in a fruitless duel. The challenger, Haliburton, fired and missed, while Howe avoided any possibility of damage by firing into the air.

Nevertheless, Joseph Howe still found it in his conscience to endorse Judge Haliburton's controversial appointment to the Supreme Court of Nova Scotia in 1841.

That same year, Haliburton's English-born wife, Louisa Neville, died after twenty-one years of marriage and eleven children.

In less than a decade between the time Sam Slick first saw the light of day and the mid-1840s, Haliburton's realization that his political ideals were doomed turned this fun-loving hedonist somewhat dour and adversely affected his writing.

Although he continued to publish until the end of his life he never again achieved the delicately balanced chaos of ambivalence that is the hallmark of great humourists. In 1849, he published *The Old Judge*, a book of observation and reminiscence revealed through the eyes of a British tourist to Nova Scotia. It has been described as a "sad book" but critics have also suggested that "in human insight and interest, it is matched only by Susanna Moodie's *Roughing It in the Bush.*

"I am too old for romance, and what is worse I am corpulent," Haliburton wrote during that period. In 1856, he resigned from the bench and moved to England. Remarried to a wealthy British widow, he was elected to the House of Commons in 1859 and distinguished himself by receiving an honorary degree from Oxford University. He never returned to Nova Scotia.

Today, Thomas C. Haliburton is seldom remembered as a jurist, historian or for his headstrong Tory ideals, but rather as an inspired humourist, the precursor of Mark Twain and Stephen Leacock. That his writing has led him to be called "the father of American humour" would probably not have surprised the author himself. After all, it was Haliburton who wrote that "truth is stranger than fiction."

In fact, Haliburton could well have referred his Yankee admirers to yet another of his Sam Slickisms: "It's a wise child that knows its own father."

PORTRAIT OF THE ARTIST AS YOUNG WOMEN

Victoria, British Columbia, 1879 — At first glance, the sepia-toned photograph looks to be nothing more than a picture of two stuffy Victorian ladies sitting for tea at a small table. One lady is primly pouring tea into a cup. The other lady looks directly into the camera, clenching her saucer. On the wall above the table there is a portrait of another woman. Or is it? There is something about the woman in the portrait. Her right arm extends outside the frame and she is pouring a full cup of tea onto the head of the lady looking obliviously into the camera. Upon even closer inspection it becomes evident that all three ladies in this photograph are one in the same person — Hannah Maynard of Mrs. R. Maynard's Photographic Gallery.

Hannah Hatherly of Cornwall, England was eighteen when she met and married apprentice bootmaker Richard Maynard in 1852. The young couple promptly sailed to Canada, where Richard opened a boot shop in Bowmanville, east of Oshawa on Lake Ontario. Six years and four children later, Richard caught "gold fever," abandoned hearth and home and joined the rush on British Columbia's Fraser River. While he was away, Hannah began studying something new and different — photography.

The daguerreotype had been invented in France in the 1830s. In 1851, Lovell's *Canada Directory* listed only eleven daguerreotypists in the country. And for one of those, photography was a second job. He listed himself as a "surgical and mechanical dentist" first, a "daguerrian artist" second.

By 1865, Mitchell & Co.'s *Canada Classified Dictionary* listed more than 360 photographers, including 34 in Montreal, 17 in Toronto and 16 in Quebec City. One among them was Mrs. Hannah Maynard of Victoria, British Columbia.

The gold fields were good to Richard Maynard. Returning to Bowmanville, he sold his shop and moved his family to Victoria in 1862. Victoria was then nothing more than a small outpost town on Vancouver Island with maybe three dozen brick buildings. In her diaries Hannah described it as a city "of tents, gullies and swamps."

Almost immediately Richard left to go prospecting up the Stikine River. Hannah settled into a house on a dirt track at the corner of Johnson and Douglas Streets and opened Mrs. R. Maynard's Photographic Gallery.

In 1863, Mr. Maynard returned to Victoria and discovered that his wife had set up her own business.

"Everyone was astonished," said a report that was printed years later in *The Colonist*. "And like many women who start anything new she was for a very long time boycotted by the public . . . until Victoria got used to a woman photographer."

Over the next fifty years it is said that Mrs. Maynard took every single resident of Victoria's portrait — usually as a baby — at least once.

Richard opened a boot store in a shop adjoining Hannah's enterprise. He must have been fascinated by Hannah's newfound career, since he was soon taking photography lessons from her. Together, Mr. and Mrs. Maynard would travel up and down the West Coast and inland through British Columbia, the Northwest Territories and Alaska, photographing the daunting and magnificent landscape. The Maynards' images were described by the *St. Louis Practical Photographer* as "the most interesting view we have ever had from those far-off regions."

Richard preferred photographing the outdoors, sometimes travelling with his eldest son, Albert. In 1868, the pair travelled by steamer and wagon to Barkerville, the terminus of the Cariboo Road. Founded six years earlier when a Cornish sailor named Billy Barker discovered gold in Williams Creek, Barkerville called itself the "largest community west of Chicago and north of San Francisco."

Although it served a population of 10,000, the "town" was little more than one muddy street lined with rough wooden shacks, a few churches and sufficient saloons to satisfy a large demand.

Richard and Albert left Barkerville on September 16, 1868, shortly before an amorous miner tried to steal a kiss from a "Hurdy Gurdy" dancehall queen who was taking some time in the afternoon to do her ironing. She resisted the miner's advances and he ended up knocking over a stovepipe. Barkerville was toast. Within an hour and twenty minutes, 116 buildings were destroyed. Maynard returned to Barkerville and photographed the desolate remains.

His images of everything from icebergs to miners clinging precariously to sheer rockfaces have an eerie stillness. At Taku Inlet, he photographed a steamer blanketed in snow and ice. In Glacier Bay, he drifted through the mist on an ice floe to capture a poetic image of two small passenger boats surrounded by chunks of ice. Government assignments and commissions saw him photographing the construction of the Canadian Pacific Railway, native people on Vancouver Island and the seal hunt in the Bering Sea.

Hannah often joined Richard on his excursions. She also travelled by herself to the Queen Charlotte Islands. However, more of her time was spent exploring commercial portraiture. She was fascinated by faces.

After plying her craft and honing her technique for almost twenty years, Hannah Maynard's eccentricity and genius began to emerge. She started to create her "Gems of British Columbia," hundreds, then thousands, of children's little faces interlocked in greeting cards.

The "gem" was a common Victorian conceit: a small and sometimes tiny tinotype featuring three or four faces of a loved one often mounted in a piece of jewellery — a ring or brooch or pendant. Producing one required a camera with four or more lenses.

Hannah became a master of such miniatures. Then she turned the whole idea on its head, producing monumental gatherings of miniatures, fields of hundreds, even thousands of tiny baby faces in montage. These gems were painstaking, artful arrangements of miniaturized portraits of every child she photographed in a given year. They are veritable fields of faces. Her 1891 "Gems of British Columbia" was framed by years of previous gems and featured approximately 22,000 faces.

She put children's faces everywhere and in everything. She would transform something as simple as a potted plant into a frenzy of leaves covered with faces. There are even faces in the potting soil. She assembled faces in frames and diamond shapes, wreaths, palettes and crosses.

In "Sprays from the Gem Fountain," sixty babies float on clouds like well-formed droplets. They emanate from a fountain composed of children blowing streams of cascading babies out of trumpets and pouring pitchers filled with babies into a reflecting pool.

Maynard also produced something else that was popular in the period called photosculptures: unwanted parts of the subject's body, such as arms below the elbow, were draped with black cloth so they became invisible to the camera. The rest of the body, especially the subject's hair, eyebrows and clothes were caked with a white powder. The result was a picture that looked like a stone bust or a ghostly sculpture. Hannah called these photographs "Living Statuary" or "Statuary from Life."

But Hannah's most adventurous work had to do with multiple images of herself such as the three ladies at tea. More magical than cut-and-paste montage or photosculpture, they reveal a sardonic woman not at all like the conventional Victorian image of womanhood. A true eccentric, intent upon herself, she displays a mocking, even gallows sense of humour.

Aside from the technical feat of her work, Hannah also took pains to paint out lines and wrinkles from her face. She was also known to "retouch" inches from her waistline.

In 1883, the Maynards' sixteen-year-old daughter Lillie died of typhoid. Images of death and the departed began to colour Hannah's work. There was a great interest in spiritualism and seances in the late nineteenth century. Even the mayor of Victoria was a spiritualist. Hannah met with spiritualists and participated in seances. Apparitions of the grotesque started to appear in her multiples.

By the mid-1890s she had moved into a visual universe all her own, achieving an aesthetic statement unmatched by photographers until the 1920s and the advent of surrealism. At the same time, she served as the official photographer for the Victoria Police Department. For five years, from 1897 until 1902, she took mug shots in her studio, sometimes using a specially designed mirror to achieve a front and side view on a single negative. Hannah retired in 1912, five years after Richard's death. She was eighty-four when she died in 1918.

Although hundreds of images created by Hannah and Richard are held in the British Columbia Archives, the work was scarcely known until Toronto artist and visual researcher Claire Weissman Wilkes discovered them while sifting through archival prints and glass plates. Wilkes's book *The Magic Box: The Eccentric Genius of Hannah Maynard*, which was published in 1980, presents a rare record of Hannah's unique vision.

"She was the real thing," writes Wilkes, "a parochial talent whose work is alive in the larger world because she was never provincial."

A GENTLEMAN
AND A SCULLER

River Thames, 1880 — When Canada's "Boy in Blue" rowed to victory, the effect was so seamless that one reporter said "his boat seemed to be pulled through the water on a string." Compact and charismatic, Edward "Ned" Hanlan became Canada's first international sports personality and the Champion Oarsman of the World.

He grew up surrounded by Lake Ontario, on the Toronto Island whose western arm now bears the name Hanlan's Point. As a child, Ned rowed across the harbour to school in a marginal craft made out of thick planks sharpened at each end. When he was five years old, he created a local sensation by threading a skiff through throngs of vessels awaiting the arrival of the Prince of Wales.

Fishermen taught him, and time spent on the water honed his skills. He was a teenager when he won his first race. After that, a blue jersey, blue shorts and a red bandanna became his uniform and a soup-strainer moustache his trademark.

Sport aside, rowing was also big business. Hanlan's talent attracted the attention of a consortium of wealthy speculators who formed the Hanlan Club in a syndicated effort to boost his championship efforts and enhance their side-betting odds. At twenty-one, Hanlan had a trainer, a sleek English shell and the latest in rowing innovations — a sliding seat and swivel oarlocks.

Crouched with his arms extended, he mastered the "slider," enhancing his stroke and relieving him of the uncomfortable buffalo skins and greased chamois pants that less technologically astute competitors used to gain extra leverage from their stationary seats.

Hanlan's syndicators had high hopes. In 1876, they entered him in the prestigious International Centennial Regatta in Philadelphia. Young Ned departed for the United States earlier than scheduled when he discovered that there was a warrant out for his arrest on charges of bootlegging. He was eventually cornered at the Toronto Rowing Club.

In a scene that could have been scripted for the Keystone Kops, Hanlan relieved the boathouse of a skiff and took off across Lake Ontario while the flat-feet stomped their heels in dry dock. A steamer filled with revellers from Toronto's German Club picked Hanlan up and he partied with them all the way to the American side of the lake.

In Philadelphia, Hanlan trained quietly with Billy McKen, a fellow-Canadian who doubled as the betting agent for the Hanlan Club. After Hanlan took the first two heats, New York gamblers are said to have been determined to prevent the young Canadian from competing. Their plot to poison Hanlan was foiled when McKen was mistaken as the target. McKen ended up drinking a doctored beer that landed him on a stretcher back to Toronto the next day. Hanlan won the race in record time and returned to the first of many celebrations in his honour. The warrant for his arrest was shredded by the chief of police.

In 1877, Hanlan won the Canadian championship. The U.S. championship followed in 1878. Hanlan outclassed all comers. During his first race in England he actually stopped to bail out his boat and still finished four lengths ahead of his rival.

He won the English championship handily, breaking the course record by fifty-two seconds. Hanlan's return to Canada was celebrated by a flotilla of yachts, sidewheelers and small craft filled with well-wishers who greeted his arrival on the steamer *Chicora* with screams, whistles and bands playing "Hail the Conquering Hero."

Match races were both crowd pleasers and big money events. In three matches with American Charles Courtney, Hanlan won thousands, but every encounter was marred by the hint of scandal. When they first raced at Lachine, Quebec in 1878, Hanlan's margin was slight and Courtney's backers claimed their man would have won if he had not accidentally strayed into Hanlan's lane.

A rematch at Chautaqua Lake in New York State attracted 50,000 spectators to the hamlet of Mayville (population: 1,000). Unbeknownst to Hanlan, some of his backers had promised Courtney a victory in the second heat. When Hanlan got wind of the plan he refused to be a party to the "fix." On the morning of the first match, Courtney's racing shell and his practise boat were discovered sawn in half.

Hanlan raced alone, covering the five-mile course in a record-breaking thirty-three minutes and fifty-six and a quarter seconds. But all bets were off and his prize money was a rubber check.

Courtney denied any impropriety on his part, leaving the world press to speculate about who was responsible. When Hanlan and Courtney met for the final time in a race on the Potomac River, Courtney claimed to have a headache and dropped out of the race.

Ned Hanlan's finest hour came on the River Thames in November, 1880. Canada's five-foot-eight-and-three-quarter-inch, 150-pound "Boy in Blue" was pitted against Australia's Edward Trickett, who was seven inches taller and fifty pounds heavier. Wagering was fierce, with half a million dollars riding on the outcome of the four-and-a-half-mile race. Torontonians alone bet $42,000 on their favourite son.

Trickett had arbitrarily declared himself the world's champion oarsman, but all of his arrogance was no match for Hanlan's prowess. A supremely confidant Hanlan took the early lead and never looked back.

Crowds lining the banks and bridges of the course cheered as he clowned his way to victory, rowing in a zig-zag pattern, blowing kisses, feigning a collapse and even pausing to chat with by standers.

Despite the debilitating effects of two bouts of typhoid, Hanlan successfully defended his world title six times over the following four years. On the international stage he was entrenched as a symbol of Canada's "muscular nationalism."

When Ned Hanlan retired from competition in 1897, he had won more than 300 races and suffered fewer than a dozen defeats. He went on to serve two terms as an alderman in Toronto and held a seat on the Toronto Harbour Trust.

The father of eight died of pneumonia in 1908 at the age of fifty-two. Eighteen years later, a towering statue of Ned Hanlan was unveiled at the Canadian National Exhibition grounds on Toronto's waterfront. It is dedicated to "the most renowned oarsman of any age whose victorious career has no parallel in the annals of sport."

THE BATTLE
OF THE BLOOMERS

Anytown, Canada, 1899 — The clergy called it the work of the devil. *Scientific American* said it might change the course of world history. Advertisements suggested it enhanced overall health and temperament. Rich and poor suffered common grief when one broke down. Women's fashion underwent a radical change.

The bicycle was a revolution in its own right. Maybe it was the consequence of having spent too much time in canoes, but velocipedes seized the Canadian imagination at the end of the nineteenth century unlike anything before or since.

Early versions featured wooden wheels. These three-wheeled "boneshakers" were soon supplanted by the English "Penny Farthing," an awkward contraption that featured an oversized front wheel. Photographs of the freshly minted Montreal Bicycle

Club circa 1878 feature throngs of mustachioed gentry astride a variety of high-wheelers. Some cycles had a small "safety" wheel at the rear, others looked more like delicate tricycles.

"Wheeling" started out as a pricey pastime. A suitable mount cost about half of the average worker's annual earnings. That did not prevent some from creating their own homemade cycles. Some early bikes where even adapted to travel on ice, with skates replacing the small back wheel.

In the 1880s, bicycle clubs became popular. Dr. J.W. "Perry" Doolittle of Toronto headed the Canadian Wheelman's Association which held its first meeting in St. Thomas, Ontario in 1881. The following year, a group of Canadian cycling enthusiasts pedalled their way to the world's fair in Chicago.

By the end of the decade, cycling was reaching a fevered pitch. Air-filled rubber tires invented by Scottish veterinarian John Dunlop in 1888 contributed to making the pastime marginally comfortable, along with the introduction of two wheels of the same diameter. Cyclists began lobbying for better roads.

In 1890, there were 17 bicycle factories in the United States. Five years later there were 300. Canadian-made bikes were assembled from imported parts until tariff legislation stopped the practice, giving rise to a homegrown industry.

In 1895, farm implement manufacturers Massey-Harris built a five-storey factory in Toronto and began churning out "Silver Ribbon" bicycles. Company president, Walter Massey, announced that: "The bicycle is not simply a fad, but it has become a thoroughly practical vehicle for use on the farm as well as in the city and in the village."

In 1896, a $16,000 shipment of Canadian bikes arrived in Australia and the following year the *New Zealand Cyclist* was reporting championship racing wins on Canadian-made racers.

Three years later, Massey-Harris joined with several other manufacturers and the Canada Cycle and Motor Company (CCM) was formed. You could get a mail-order bicycle for twenty-five dollars.

A small industry grew up around the bicycle. Cycling clubs published hotel guides for wheeling tourists. Accessories included everything from goggles to gaiters. Cycling academies urged that "ladies intending to wheel cannot do better than register at once before it becomes too crowded."

The bicycle was an instrument of liberation for women. Whalebone corsets and crinolines fell by the wayside, and chaperones simply could not keep up the pace.

Women wearing "bifurcated nether garments" commonly known as "Bloomers" were decried in *Saturday Night* magazine for the sin of revealing "the most shapeless lot of legs ever seen outside a butcher shop." A lady's bicycle suit with a shortened skirt and cycling tights sold for about fifteen dollars.

"Six or seven years ago there were no lady cyclists in Canada. Can you fancy it, my sisters?" Grace Denison wrote in an 1896 article titled "The Evolution of the Lady Cyclist."

"In one short demi-decade we have learned a new enthusiasm, gone through the battle of the bloomer, and taken into our lives a new pleasure, the like of which we never before experienced or even in our dreams imagined."

Bicycles were everywhere. Doctors pedalled to deliver babies. Telegrams were delivered by bicycle courier. Everything from policing to postal service incorporated cycling. Hotels hired bellboys to park their guest bicycles and managers of fine dining rooms complained about the "loud body sweat and road perfume" of their cycling clients.

A six-day workweek meant making careful decisions about managing one's recreational time. Piano sales decreased. Tavern owners found themselves idle when their clientele took to spending weekends riding into the country for picnics. Church attendance dropped severely, particularly during the summer. In 1894, a minister in Kingston, Ontario railed against the "monkeyback" posture of cyclists who crouched at the handlebars and raised their rumps for a streamlining effect.

On the prairies it was said that bands of cyclists looked "like birds on a telegraph wire." But surely the oddest application of the bicycle involved those hearty fools who joined the Klondike gold rush on their bikes. In the winter of 1897, two New Yorkers got as far as the foot of White Pass near Skagway in the Yukon. They were travelling on two bicycles that were joined by iron bars, which in turn supported a canoe containing their gear.

Bicycle races attracted thousands of spectators and prizes ranged from a six-room house to handfuls of uncut diamonds. At the first annual Dunlop Trophy Race in 1894, winner Tom McCarthy was estimated to achieve a top speed of twelve miles per hour.

The bicycle frenzy peaked in 1899 when Montreal hosted the world cycling championship.

The following year, Archie McEachern became the first Canadian to win the twenty-five-mile indoor championship in Boston.

Racing teams included the Brantford Red Birds, and featured professional race champions like Harley Davidson, who bore no relation to the founding fathers of the American motorcycle company.

Despite the automobile's conquest of the road-ways, bicycle races remained popular throughout the 1920s. At the 1928 Olympics in Amsterdam, Canadian hopes were riding on a twenty-two-year-old racer from Victoria, B.C. who was built like a football player. Red-haired William "Torchy" Peden started the 100-mile Olympic endurance competition, but he was foiled by two punctured tires. The following year, Torchy swept the Canadian indoor championships.

Then he turned professional and embarked on a racing career that made him an international celebrity.

Six-day races were the rage during the Depression, bringing in more than a quarter of a million dollars a week. Pairs of racers took turns lapping a track non-stop for 144 hours. In the tradition of marathon dances, best and brutally epitomized in the 1969 movie *They Shoot Horses, Don't They*, six-day races were gruelling affairs.

Often paired with his brother Doug "Tiny" Peden, Torchy excelled as a "sixer," and crowds marvelled at his sheer power. His trainer called him: "Muscles with a smile." To alleviate boredom, Torchy would ride on one knee or grab women's hats and tear around the track. Between 1931 and 1942, Peden won thirty-eight six-day races and his name was as well-known as baseball's Babe Ruth.

In the off-season, vacant hockey arenas were often used for six-day races. Peden started his career at the Montreal Forum. When races were held on outdoor tracks, the competitors lived in makeshift huts on the infield, never far from their bicycles.

It was a world that went round and round, slowing only during the wee hours of the morning, but never stopping. When crowds were on hand, racers would engage in sprints and jams for cash prizes. A sprint was a ten-lap dash, a jam was a team spurt.

Racers were rarely off the track for more than half an hour. They took catnaps, even while they were riding. Crashes were often spectacular. Peden is said to have fallen asleep once while doing a lap and he ended up taking a header that landed him over the boards and straight into his ringside bunk, just as though he had planned it.

Fads pass and cycling lost its glamour, only to be rediscovered by the children of post-World War II baby boomers.

After all, learning to ride is simple. It's as easy as falling off a bicycle.

THE COWBOY FROM QUEBEC

The West, 1930 — He said he was an only child, born under a wagon in Montana. He also said that his mother died when he was a year old, leaving his Texas cowboy father to raise him, until an encounter with a long-horned steer left the child an orphan.

In fact, he was born in St. Nazaire, Quebec in 1892. He had two brothers and three sisters. His mother was still living in 1934, when he visited the family home in Montreal for the express purpose of destroying every-thing that could link his true identity to the fantastic fraud that he had created.

Joseph Ernest Nephtali Dufault had many aliases, but the one that finally stuck was "Will James." He was a bestselling author, a cowboy contemporary of Will Rogers and Tom Mix, and an illustrator whose detailed sketches of horses were so lifelike that one critic suggested they "seem to leap from the page and kick dirt all over you."

Even though his autobiography *Lone Cowboy: My Life Story* ranked fifth on the non-fiction best-sellers list in 1930, one of the few non-fiction events described by its author concerned his 1914 arrest for cattle rustling.

"I often wish that I hadn't misrepresented myself as I did," Dufault/James confessed in a letter to his brother Auguste, "but I couldn't dream of the success I've had and now it's too late to change."

The greenhorn from Montreal with a Grade Eight education spent his entire adult life pretending he was "born and raised in the cow country."

He successfully deceived his wife, his publisher and his faithful readers, but the strain of deception took its toll. At the age of fifty, he died alone and broke in a Hollywood hospital of cirrhosis of the liver and kidney failure caused by alcoholism.

The groundwork for the invention of "Will James" began in 1907, when fifteen-year-old Ernest Dufault talked his parents into providing a one-way ticket to Regina. Fascinated by the lore and lifestyle of the West, he spent the remainder of his teenage years learning about ranch life and honing his cowboy skills.

He also learned English. A fellow Québécois named Beaupre is thought to have been his mentor. At one point, both men filed homestead claims at Val Marie near the Cypress Hills which spans the Alberta/Saskatchewan border. Later, in his infamous autobiography, Will James wrote that as an orphaned child, a family friend "Bopy" (Beaupre) adopted him and raised him.

In the book, the kindly French-Canadian trapper teaches the boy to hunt during the Canadian winters and shows him the ways of the cowboy during summers in Montana.

According to James's story, Bopy drowns in the ice-filled Red Deer River, leaving his protégé to fend for himself with a lingering French accent that could be easily explained without revealing the truth.

By the time he reached his early twenties, the lanky, dark-haired vagabond had worked at many of Western Canada's largest ranches and drifted around Montana, Idaho, Wyoming and New Mexico. He tried on various aliases that sounded more authentically "western" than Dufault, including Clint Jackson, Stonewall and William Roderick James.

In 1914, "Bill James" was riding bucking horses at a small rodeo in Medicine Hat where fellow cowboy Ronald "Crying" Mason noted that "Bill was as good a bronc rider" as he had ever seen.

That same year a botched cattle rustling attempt earned the self-described "Montana-born" Will James a fifteen-month sentence in the Nevada State Prison at Carson City.

After serving his time, James resumed the cowboy life. He also worked as a stuntman and extra in Hollywood westerns.

In 1917, when he was visiting friends in Calgary, he ended up driving around the Prairies in a Model T Ford that he covered in crayon drawings of bucking horses. As a part of a loose cowboy street show featuring the likes of Sleepy Epperson on harmonica and Calgary Red serving up roping tricks, James was the announcer, known as "Bullshit Bill."

From childhood, he had always enjoyed drawing images of Western life, and his hands-on experience wrangling horses, herding cattle and living the bunkhouse life gave his drawings authenticity. When he was sidelined with a concussion after a tumble from a bucking horse, a fellow patient noticed his flair for drawing and provided a letter of introduction to an editor at the popular San Francisco illustrated magazine *Sunset*.

James attempted to study art seriously at the California School of Fine Arts in San Francisco and he was offered a scholarship to Yale University. However, his inspiration came from memory, and formal studies did not suit him.

Sunset magazine published a series of his drawings in 1920, and New York's leading illustrated magazine, *Scribner's*, invited him to submit stories with his drawings.

With the encouragement of his teenaged wife, Alice, James wrote and illustrated "Bucking Horses and Bucking-Horse Riders," in one week and pronounced it "too easy done to be any good."

Scribner's paid him $300 and James became a regular contributor, with seven feature stories appearing in 1923.

"I am a cowboy, and what's put down in these pages is not material that I've hunted up, it's what I've lived, seen and went thru before I ever had any idea that my writing and sketches would ever appear before the public," James wrote in the preface to his first book, *Cowboys North and South*. Bad grammar and all, it was his unique "cowboyese" language and intimate understanding of the actual life of cowboys that separated James from the "pulp western" writers of the era. His work was celebrated for its literary achievement, which the *New York Times* described as "unvarnished but singularly salty and effective."

In 1927, his third book, *Smoky, The Cowhorse* won the coveted Newbery Medal for Children's Literature. It was translated into at least six foreign languages and became the subject of three motion picture treatments. On the strength of *Smoky*'s success, his publisher advanced James money to buy a ranch near Billings, Montana.

Between 1924 and 1942, Will James published twenty-four books, but his life seems to have begun to unravel after the publication of his autobiography.

One of his biographers, Anthony Amaral, noted that in the aftermath of *Lone Cowboy* James's "career and his integrity were balanced on a precarious suppression of his true credentials."

In 1935, a year after the film version of *Lone Cowboy* premiered and a year after he returned to Canada to destroy any lingering trace of his true identity in the

Dufault home, his wife, Alice, left. In 1936, James lost the Rocking R Ranch to his creditors. Years of excessive drinking and fear of discovery finally eroded his health and his talent.

Although romanticized, Will James's work is acknowledged to be among the finest examples of cowboy art ever produced. A collection of his work, including a striking self-portrait with Stetson, is permanently displayed at the Yellowstone Art Center, and singer-song writer Ian Tyson is one of James's avid Canadian collectors.

Like his contemporary, literary fraud Archibald Belaney who gained fame and notoriety as the Canadian Indian author Grey Owl, the secret truth of Will James's identity was not revealed until after his death. It passed without much notice in his homeland.

Half a century later, a society dedicated to Will James was formed. It meets once a year somewhere in North America where the cowboy from Quebec is known to have lassoed a calf, tamed a bronco or sketched a tumbleweed.

Medicine Hat educator and freelance curator Allan Jensen, who has served on the Board of Directors of the Will James Society, notes: "As Canadians, we need to repatriate Will James, his legend and his legacy as part of our cultural property and heritage."

A MAN IN A HURRY

Ottawa, 1939 — "In a film you must tell a story, otherwise you are boring," John Grierson once told a gathering of students in Montreal.

The man who has been called "the father of documentary film," was himself never boring. Likewise, the stories he aided and abetted in telling as the first head of the National Film Board of Canada were never boring. The mandate was to tell Canadians about their country and inform the world about Canada.

Grierson was a child of modest privilege, growing up in Scotland as the son of two accomplished educators. He studied philosophy at Glasgow University and served a stint on a minesweeper during the First World War.

A Rockefeller Foundation Fellowship brought him to America where he studied social science and the effects of mass media. His specialty soon became propaganda, which he considered to be an educational tool.

"We can by propaganda, widen the horizons of the schoolroom and give to every individual, each in his place and work, a living conception of the community which he has the privilege to serve," Grierson once noted.

Grierson spent a decade in England, where he organized a government film unit. In 1929, he produced and directed *Drifters*, a film about the harsh and dangerous circumstances of herring fishermen in the North Sea. It became a model for British documentaries, featuring a style Grierson summed up as "working men with their sleeves rolled up."

Grierson is said to have coined the term *documentary* in response to the filmmaking techniques of Robert Flaherty, who turned his lens on the daily life of the Inuit in 1922 to create *Nanook of the North*.

By 1938, Grierson was acknowledged to be an expert in the field of documentary film production which he liked to call "the creative interpretation of reality."

The Canadian government under Prime Minister William Lyon Mackenzie King asked Grierson to come to Canada to draft a plan for a government film unit. On May 2, 1939, what became known as the National Film Board of Canada was created by an Act of Parliament, and Grierson was appointed its director shortly afterwards.

When Canada entered the Second World War, Grierson also became the manager of the Wartime

Information Board. As Canada's "propaganda maestro," he embarked on an energetic program, including a monthly series of short films that were shown in theatres across the country.

Canada Carries On highlighted the influence ordinary Canadians had on the war effort, along with strategies and themes that placed the Canadian effort in a global context. *Food for Thought* offered nutritional information in times of food shortage. *Women Are Warriors* showed English, Russian and Canadian women serving on the front lines and in factory lines. The *Strategy of Metals* pitted Canada's aluminum resources and manufacturing against a backdrop of German armaments.

Along with churning out pleas for war bond support, there was some straight-up propaganda such as the anti-Japanese film *The Mark of Nippon*, which bore the French title *Les Nazis jaunes*.

Many of these documentaries became a part of another series, *World in Action*, which reached an international audience of more than thirty million viewers.

In 1941, barely two years after its formation, the National Film Board of Canada won its first Academy Award for *Churchill's Island*. While illustrating the Battle of Britain, the film also focused on British civilians holding fast in the face of war with "stubborn calm." The last line: "Come — if you dare," intoned by Canada's "Voice of Doom" narrator Lorne Greene, spoke directly to John Grierson's aspiration to see the Americans join the war. Six months later, they did. "Art is not a mirror, it is a hammer," was another Grierson saying.

In the six years that Grierson served at the NFB, hundreds of films were made by a team of more than 800 filmmakers. The hive of all of this activity was an aged sawmill on John Street in Ottawa, where a barn served as both screening room and recording studio. Despite the fact that the occupants of the elegant French embassy across the road considered the NFB building a blight, composer and conductor Louis Applebaum was occasionally able to cajole them into allowing rehearsal time on their superior piano.

During the Second World War film was rationed, but with Grierson's blessing independent film producers continued to work — for the NFB.

Years later, Academy Award–winning independent film producer and director Budge Crawley (*The Man Who Skied Down Everest*) recalled the importance of Grierson to development of the film industry in Canada. "Grierson employed all of the country's film skills to do what he thought were useful things," he told a Grierson symposium in 1981. "He always encouraged us. He gave us recruiting films. I spent months moving little Dinky-Toy tanks around and making tank training films."

Grierson also imported talent to get the Film Board up and running. In 1941, Grierson asked a fellow Scot, animator Norman McLaren, to join the NFB. *V for Victory* (1941) was the first of many short McLaren war effort pieces.

Ultimately, McLaren founded an animation department at the Film Board and became world-renowned for his experimental and lyrically poetic animated films.

Grierson left the NFB under an unpleasant cloud raised by the Cold War. Rumours of a "Communist nest" at the NFB were fanned when a reference to an NFB secretary was discovered in evidence that Soviet cipher clerk Igor Gouzenko turned over to the RCMP as proof of a spy ring operating out of the Soviet embassy. A Royal Commission ensued, implying that Grierson had knowingly hired Communists and allowed them to flourish at the NFB. He resigned in 1945.

"In all the RCMP files about Grierson there was not one thing said to implicate him, except through Freda Linton. She was his secretary . . . there was nothing to tar his name," an RCMP security officer said later.

Grierson had planned to go to America and start an independent film company after the war ended. However, this plan was foiled by Federal Bureau of Investigation director J. Edgar Hoover who targeted Grierson in the midst of the "red scare." U.S. newspapers crowed "Spy Suspect Expelled" when Grierson's visa was revoked in 1947.

After a brief stint with UNESCO in Paris, Grierson returned to Britain. He became controller of the Central Office of Information and guided a government film finance corporation designed to foster new talent, including Kenneth More, Peter Finch and Peter Sellers.

Despite recurrent bouts with tuberculosis, Grierson remained active. At home in Scotland, the self-described "man in a hurry," worked on the Oscar-winning *Seawards the Great Ships*. From 1957 to 1967, he was the host of *This Wonderful World*, a documentary television series produced for a Scottish television station owned by Canadian press magnate Lord Thomson of Fleet.

In 1968, Grierson was invited to lecture at Montreal's McGill University, where he held some of his seminars on filmmaking at his apartment.

"Something *does* something *to* something," he told students. "You must reveal the secret of that interaction, whether it is a psychological story, a political story or a story about tying shoe-laces."

Never stumped for an opinion, Grierson also postulated that, "People with eight mm minds shouldn't make thirty-five mm films."

As Grierson's biographer, H. Forsyth Harvy, noted, "He was never happier in his life than when he was bombarding complacency."

The "father of documentary film" died in England in 1972 at the age of seventy-three. Honours were heaped on Grierson during his lifetime, but the only one he almost received from Canada — an honorary doctorate from McGill — arrived posthumously. In 1973, the Grierson Building of the NFB in Montreal was dedicated in his memory.

The energy, elegance and intelligent "eye" that was Grierson's legacy to Canadian culture has earned the National Film Board more than 3,000 national and international awards.

In 1989, the NFB was celebrated with an Academy Award in recognition of its first fifty years. Despite recent restructuring and downsizing (which critics have called "gutting"), the NFB continues to produce an average of 100 uniquely Canadian films every year.

"There is a profound element of common sense and good taste about Canada and Canadian life which is a precious thing to know," Grierson wrote. "This the Film Board reflects and demonstrates."

SPONTANEOUS COMBUSTION

Montreal, 1948 — Few Canadians have ever heard of *Refus global*, a pastiche of diatribe, essay and screed written by a group of French-Canadian artists and first published in Montreal on August 6, 1948.

"Published" is a bit of a misnomer: 400 mimeographed copies of the 100-page document with a cover drawn by Jean-Paul Riopelle were distributed among family and friends.

Separatists and other free thinkers in Quebec have long since seized upon *Refus global* as an unofficial founding document. Certain academics and intellectuals ruefully cite it as the opening salvo in Quebec's Quiet Revolution.

In 1998, on the fiftieth anniversary of its appearance, *Refus global* —in English, "universal refusal" or "total rejection" — became the celebrated subject of exhibitions, films, radio documentaries and conferences all over the country.

The Post Office even issued a series of stamps based on paintings by a variety of contributors to the obscure manifesto, including works by Riopelle, Pierre Gavreau, Fernand Leduc, Marcel Barbeau, and the *Refus global*'s driving force, Paul-Émile Borduas, who is by now torqued by the irrepressible irony of it all, spinning furiously in his grave.

What would the brilliant painter who died an exile in Paris at the age of fifty-four, thirty-eight years before this anniversary, make of the fact that the publication that ruined the life he cherished, was now a *cause célèbre*?

A month after the release of *Refus global*, Borduas received a letter informing him that the Minister of Social Welfare and Youth for Quebec had demanded that he be dismissed "because the writings and manifestos he had published, as well as his general attitude, are not of a kind to favour the teaching we wish to provide our students."

And so Borduas, a distinguished, well-liked and eminently qualified teacher, was summarily dismissed from École du Meuble in Montreal, from a job he not only liked but desperately needed.

For his role in organizing, editing and writing the seminal essay in *Refus global* Borduas was not only fired, but denounced from the pulpit as a sinner and called a madman in the press.

Although Borduas' paintings continued to sell, the income was no where near enough to support him and his family. His wife, a devout Catholic, took their three young children and went home to her mother

"We must break with the conventions of society once and for all, and reject its utilitarian spirit. We must refuse to function knowingly at less than our physical and mental potential," Borduas youthfully enthused in *Refus global*:

> Refuse to close our eyes to vice and fraud perpetrated in the name of knowledge or favours or due respect. . . . We refuse to keep silent. Do what you want with us, but you must hear us out. We will not accept your fame or attendant honours. They are the stigmata of shame, silliness and servility. We refuse to serve, or to be used for such purposes. . . . MAKE WAY FOR MAGIC! MAKE WAY FOR OBJECTIVE MYSTERIES! MAKE WAY FOR LOVE! MAKE WAY FOR THE INTERNAL DRIVES!

In retrospect, *Refus global* seems innocent, ardent and rhapsodic. Uneven and sometimes naive, it is exactly the sort of thing one might expect from a group of young, diverse artists that included experimental poet Claude Gauvreau, painters such as the now world-famous Riopelle, dancer/choreographers including Jeanne Renaud and Françoise Sullivan, and Marcelle Ferron, who created the spectacular stained-glass window for the Champs de Mars station.

The writings that sacked Borduas also earned him and his fellow contributors, many of whom were his students, police dossiers.

Believe it or not, as a consequence of *Refus global*, most of the young men and women who were signatories to the document came under surreptitious RCMP surveillance, which, in some cases, quietly lasted their lifetime. Considered subversives, they lost jobs and suffered social ostracism.

A young journalist named Tancred Marsil writing in a magazine called *Quartier Latin*, dubbed the group "*les automatistes*," a moniker meant to describe their idealization of creative spontaneity.

Philosophically, the manifesto of *les automatistes* has a great deal in common with the sentiments and attitudes that informed Jack Kerouac's *On the Road*, which, although written in the late 1940s, was not published until 1957.

Kerouac, a contemporary of Borduas, was the son of French-Canadian immigrants who hailed from the same countryside as Borduas' family before moving to Lowell, Massachusetts. While Borduas became a pariah, Kerouac became the philosopher-king of the "beat" generation, a generation that lionized the outsider.

Unlike *On the Road*, *Refus global* really had little or no impact on anyone except its creators. Published anywhere other than Quebec in the late 1940s, *Refus global* would have either been ignored, quietly indulged or mildly celebrated by the intelligentsia.

But it could not be tolerated by the retrograde cabinet of Premier Maurice Duplessis, controlled as it was by the staid, nineteenth-century mores of the Catholic Church. As Clarke Blaise observes in his memoir, *I Had A Father*, French Canadians were possessed of "a garrison mentality, afraid to venture forth, suspicious of outsiders, always defensive about the loss of language, culture and religion."

Garrison mentalities tend to treat usurpers, intellectual or otherwise, rather badly. And thus befell Borduas his fate, a kind of sweet oblivion.

Sweet because, although lonely, homesick and ill at the end of his short life, his art had long been recognized and rewarded for what it was — brilliant. And Borduas' last years in Paris were among his most interesting and productive.

Ironically, cultural life in Montreal during the late forties and fifties was by far the most cosmopolitan and sophisticated, outside of New York, on the North American continent. By comparison, Toronto was Hicksville. Despite the pervasive machinations of the narrow-minded Catholic junta that defined the status quo and kept Duplessis in power, it was visceral, which is why Borduas loved it so.

Paradoxically, at the centre of the orgiastic, free-thinking exposition that eventually propelled Borduas out of wedlock and la belle province was a rather worldly, expatriate, French Dominican priest named Father Alain Couturier.

In New York when the war broke, fate and the good Lord sent Father Alain north to Montreal. After

God and the Virgin Mary, Father Couturier was most dedicated to the doctrine of the new, particularly in the world of art and ideas. Once entrenched, he proceeded to make a career out of disturbing fecal matter in Montreal's vibrant cultural community.

Publicly criticizing École des Beaux-Arts, the establishment art school in Montreal that Borduas had attended as a youth, Father Couturier regularly fed *les automatistes* provocative sermon/lectures on cubism, surrealism and dada.

In 1940, the Quebec-born artist Pellan, who had been living in Paris, came home in full plumage with his enthusiasms, his startling, surrealistic paintings, his books and his intimate knowledge of Braque, Picasso and their precursors.

Fernand Leger, passing through the city in 1943, gave a lecture and showed his famous, ground-breaking film *Le Ballet mecanique*.

In 1944, a travelling exhibition of Dutch paintings, including those of Mondrian, were revelations to Borduas and *les automatistes*.

One of the signatories to *Refus global*, Fernand Leduc, made contact with Andre Breton in New York. The leader of the French Surrealist Movement invited *les automatistes* to formally align itself with Surrealism, an invitation that, in the spirit of *Refus global*, was politely refused.

In 1947 the group was again invited by a persistent Breton to take part in an International Surrealist

Exhibition in Paris. Although they once again declined, it is an indication that there was nothing parochial or provincial about the art scene in Montreal.

Borduas was himself classically trained. He began his career as apprentice to the last, and arguably the greatest Church painter Canada has ever known, Ozias Leduc.

Leduc (1864–1955), who lived like a recluse in Saint Hilaire, has a special place in Canadian art. Not only did he paint remarkable religious murals and altars that still define and dominate dozens of churches throughout Quebec, but he also painted radiant still lifes that were inspirational to the development of modern painting in Canada.

An excellent student and apprentice, Borduas then went to École des Beaux-Arts in Montreal and from there, on to Paris where he studied at the École d'Art Sacrés, the most important centre for ecclesiastic art in France.

After losing his job and his marriage, Borduas moved to New York where abstract expressionists such as Jackson Pollack and Mark Rothko were flourishing. By 1954, Borduas' work was included in the collection at the Museum of Modern Art.

That same year he moved to Europe, eventually settling in Paris, never to return to his beloved Quebec. Over the next twenty years he painted feverishly and produced a body of work that is among the finest in Canadian history. His paintings are characterized by the way he piled layer upon layer of paint on canvas, rich, tactile flourishes, using knives and trowels.

In Paris he was a great success. He had many dealers and museums asking for his work all over the world. Not only did Paul-Émile Borduas survive, he thrived.

His daughter, Renée, who only saw her father twice after he moved to Paris, has said that after her father left she "started talking" to his paintings.

"For me the best was there. . . . So it was my job to listen to it, to understand it, to get close to it if I could."

About the austere, powerful black and white paintings produced in the last year of his life and now considered Borduas' masterpieces, his daughter said that she came to see them as the "supreme attempt to reconcile what was not reconcilable."

"He has taken extremes and made them co-exist with one another. He has made them sing. . . . He's showed us the way it can be done."

MORE STARS THAN HEAVEN

Hollywood, California 1900s to Present — During the Depression the son of a Russian émigré who grew up in Saint John, New Brunswick was the highest paid executive in the United States and one of the most powerful men in Hollywood.

Eliezer (Lazar) Mayer's father worked as a junk dealer and his mother sold chickens door-to-door. Their son was three when they arrived in Canada in 1888, after suffering from repeated anti-Jewish pogroms.

Three decades later, Eliezer would be famous as Louis B. (Burt) Mayer, also known as "Louis the Conqueror." He was the third "M" in the Metro-Goldwyn-Mayer Studio, whose slogan "more stars than there are in the heavens" was a virtual reality in the 1930s. Greta Garbo, Judy Garland, Jean Harlow and Clark Gable were among the stars shaped by MGM, under the patriarchal and sometimes tyrannical guidance of Louis Mayer.

L.B. Mayer was not the only Hollywood mogul with a Canadian connection whose name graced a California film studio during those early and heady days of the motion picture industry. Danville, Quebec's Mikall Sinnott transformed himself into Mack Sennett, and produced the first full-length, silent comedy motion picture *Tillie's Punctured Romance* in 1914 through his studio, Keystone Productions.

Sennett was thrown for a loop by the advent of "talking pictures." That phenomenon was pioneered by the Warner Brothers — Sam, Harry, Albert and Jack — whose Warner Bros. studio launched *The Jazz Singer* in 1927.

Like Louis B. Mayer's family, the Warners emigrated to North America to escape the persecution of czarist Russia. Their father, Benjamin, was a peddler and the family travelled extensively before settling in Youngstown, Ohio around the turn of the century. The youngest Warner child, Jack, earned his Canadian connection by being born in London, Ontario in 1892.

Both Louis B. Mayer and the brothers Warner entered the world of cinema from the popcorn side rather than the creative side. As the story goes, in 1904, the Warners sold the family delivery horse and bought a film projector. The following year, the brothers opened a "hole-in-the-wall" nickelodeon theatre in Newcastle, Pennsylvania. Louis B. Mayer, who had moved to Boston in his late teens, also bought a run-down theatre.

While Mayer decided to renovate his theatre and expanded his business into the largest theatre chain in New England, the Warners decided to become film distributors. By the 1920s, they were all making movies in sunny California.

There was something of a "six degrees of separation" syndrome in the early years of Hollywood. Canadian-connected Louis B. Mayer relied heavily on the brilliance of his production chief, Irving Thalberg, to guide MGM. Thalberg was married to Montreal-born Norma Shearer. Norma's brother, Douglas, the head of MGM's sound department for forty years, earned himself a dozen Academy Awards.

In 1959, Douglas Shearer received a special Oscar as co-developer of MGM's wide-screen camera system. Also honoured at the 1959 Academy Awards was Jack L. Warner, recipient of the Irving G. Thalberg Memorial Award. In 1999, the Thalberg Award was presented to Toronto-born, internationally renowned director Norman Jewison.

Of course, none of these awards would have existed if Louis B. Mayer had not suggested the idea in 1927. It was a concept that was heartily endorsed by actor Douglas Fairbanks, husband of "America's Sweetheart" Toronto-born actress Mary Pickford, both of whom were founding members of the Academy of Motion Picture Arts and Sciences.

In fact, Mary Pickford was a mogul in her own right. In 1920 she and Fairbanks founded Universal

Pictures, along with the popular "little tramp" Charlie Chaplin, who had been discovered by Mack Sennett.

Acting under the pseudonym "Dorothy Nicholson," golden-haired Mary (whose real name was Gladys Marie Smith) made her first film under director D.W. Griffith in 1908. One of her co-stars was Mack Sennett, who also took the odd acting job, having been mentored in vaudeville by Coburg-born Marie Dressler.

D.W. Griffith went on to make the legendary *The Birth of a Nation* in 1915, and it was the success of the ticket receipts from that film that skyrocketed Louis B. Mayer from the popcorn side of cinema to the production side.

Sam Warner probably deserves the title "Father of the Talking Picture" because it was his idea to use synchronized sound in movies. His brother Harry was leery at first.

"Who the hell wants to hear actors talk?" Harry asked.

Sam never lived to find out. He died the day before *The Jazz Singer*'s debut in New York City.

The star of the picture, Al Jolson, went on to fame and fortune. In 1933, while making the Warner Brothers' musical *42nd Street*, Jolson met his future wife, Halifax-born hoofer Ruby Keeler. Thirty-three years later, Ruby showed up as an extra in *They Shoot Horses, Don't They*, starring Montreal's Michael Sarrazin.

Also in 1933, Hollywood chose a Canadian to grace an ape's palm. Alberta-born Fay Wray was twenty-six when she was mauled by the movie's most famous monkey, King Kong. Twenty-one years later, New Westminster, B.C.'s Raymond (William Stacy) Burr also shared billing with an overblown primate in *Gorilla at Large*.

In 1957, Wray and Burr were united in *The Case of the Fatal Fetish* and an early television episode of Perry Mason.

Doctors were larger-than-life in Dr. Kildare, a TV series featuring young Richard Chamberlain operating under the watchful eye of Raymond Massey as Dr. Gillespie. Massey first trod the boards of a stage at Oakville, Ontario's upper-crust Appleby College. He earned a 1941 Oscar nomination playing an American politician in *Abe Lincoln in Illinois*, which co-starred London, Ontario's Gene Lockhart.

A dozen years later, Raymond Massey's brother, Vincent, was appointed as the first Canadian-born Governor General of Canada. At the time, Raymond was on the big screen playing a prophet in the steamy biblical film *David and Bathsheba*.

Regina-born Erik and Leslie Nielsen represent another famous politician/actor combination that flew about as high as it gets. Erik served in the federal Cabinet, while his brother was buffooning somewhere between *Airplane!* and *Naked Gun*. Early in Leslie's career he played the romantic lead in *Tammy and the Bachelor*. Fay Wray was cast as his mother.

Actresses Beatrice Lillie (born in Toronto), Deanna Durbin (Winnipeg), Alexis Smith (Penticton, B.C.) and

Yvonne De Carlo (Vancouver) are only a few degrees of separation apart from many other Canadians in Hollywood.

For instance, Deanna Durbin received a juvenile Academy Award in 1939 for her contribution as a "personification of youth." She shared the award with Mickey Rooney, who was at the peak of his fame starring in Louis B. Mayer's *Andy Hardy* films. In a dozen films Cecilia Parker (born in 1905 in Fort Williams, Ontario) played Andy Hardy's big sister.

Whether as moguls or bit players, Canadians have always been "in the movies," separated by just a few degrees.

In 1992, Ottawa-born Dan Ackroyd appeared in *Chaplin*, a film about some of the early days in Hollywood when Mary Pickford was the queen of the screen. He played Mack Sennett.

And, even in death, Louis B. Mayer and the Warner brothers are not far apart.

All are resting at the Home of Peace Memorial Park in Los Angeles, California.

Heroes, Heroines
&
the Odd Scoundrel

AN UNAMERICAN HERO

SINK OR SWIM

WHITE LAMA

THE GREAT STORK DERBY

A BELLY LAUGH OR YOUR MONEY BACK

A MALTESE FALCON

"DON'T LET THE CRIPPLED KIDS DOWN"

AN UNAMERICAN HERO

Stoney Creek, Upper Canada, 1813 — Canadian author/humorist Eric Nichol has noted that: "Very little is known about the War of 1812 because the Americans lost it." Maybe that is why so few Americans know that during that war, British troops burned the White House in Washington, D.C. as retaliation for American action in Niagara, York (Toronto) and in Upper Canada.

What some Americans have in retrospect characterized as a mere "border skirmish," was in fact a full-blown, often poorly executed, American attempt at the conquest of a peaceful people. In its failure, settlers north of the 49th parallel developed an appreciation of the nature of their budding nationhood and a determination not to be American.

The turning point in the conflict occurred in the pre-dawn hours of June 6, 1813. One of the heroes of the battle, which pitted 700 British troops against 2,000 invaders, was a civilian teenager named Billy Green.

William Green is said to have been the first white child born in Saltfleet Township near Stoney Creek. Born in a log cabin on February 4, 1794, he was the eleventh child of Loyalists Adam and Martha Green who had abandoned their 6,000-acre New Jersey holdings to accept a grant of 300 acres of bush on the Niagara Escarpment. Mrs. Green died shortly after the birth and young Billy was raised by his older sisters.

By all accounts, including legend, Billy grew up attuned to his environment, ranging freely through forests of pine, oak and elm as an adventurous loner and a natural woodsman. The local people called him "Billy the Scout," and he made use of his knowledge as a member of the Fifth Lincoln militia unit.

Billy was on a wooded ridge trail with his older brother, Levi, in the early morning of June 5, 1813. From their vantage point, they saw blue-coated regiments of American soldiers, including light infantry and cavalry marching toward the village of Stoney Creek at noon. The Americans were two days' march away from their headquarters at Fort George on the Niagara River, which they had taken from the British just days earlier.

Whooping like Indians, Billy and Levi set off to warn the settlers, including Levi's wife and their sister, Keziah Corman. When they reached the Cormans' farm, they learned that Keziah's husband, Isaac, had been taken prisoner by the enemy who had been asking questions about the location of Indian camps.

Fearing the worst, Billy went off in search of his brother-in-law, but miraculously Isaac turned up unharmed. Kentucky-born Corman had apparently secured his release by telling his captors that he was a relative of American General William Henry Harrison. The officer in charge was so impressed that when he released Corman he gave him a password that would allow him to move freely through enemy lines.

The countersign phrase is said to have been "Will-Har-Hen," based on the first three syllables of the American General's name. Billy knew that this would be vital information to the British, who were encamped at Burlington Heights about ten kilometres away. He was determined to deliver the message.

Sentries were already patrolling the main road that Billy had to cross with the password that should have presented no problem, but at that precise and critical moment Billy Green had a stunning lapse of memory.

"I forgot it," he admitted years later. Not knowing what to do, Billy improvised a disguise. "I pulled my coat over my head and trotted across the road on my feet and hands like a bear."

Back at Levi's house on the hillside, he mounted his brother's horse, Tip, and rode as far as he could toward the British encampment. He finished the mountainous climb on foot, arriving an hour before midnight.

The British were aware of the American troop movement, but Billy was able to provide detailed information and he knew the countryside like the back of his hand. A night attack was quickly scheduled.

With Billy serving as guide, the advance party made its way toward the American camp without so much as moonlight to guide them. There was sheet lightning over the lake and a brief shower made the going muddy and difficult. Two British regiments, under General John Vincent and Colonel John Harvey, were instructed to remove the flints from their muskets to avoid the accidental discharge of weapons. The initial attack was to be a "cold steel exercise" — a silent surprise to the sleeping Americans.

Accounts vary; however, it seems that by the time the advance group reached the first sentry, Billy Green had recovered the memory of the password and used it to get close enough to the man for a bayonet to silence him. Another guard was dispatched in a similar fashion. Only when a third sentry managed to fire off a shot while he drowned in his own blood did the Americans wake up. By that time, a church containing thirty guards had been captured while they slept in the pews.

Bayonets fixed, the British proceeded to enter the American camp. Whooping like Indians they found themselves in the midst of the dying campfires of the regimental mess, confronting a few early bird cooks and tripping over sundry cookware. One local history suggests that the Americans must have thought they had been "attacked by the entire British army and surrounded by all the Indians in Canada." The element of surprise was lost.

The Americans had been sleeping on a hill, with their loaded weapons at their sides. Before the British could fix their flints, the Americans were firing on them. For a time, disorder prevailed. Orders to the British troops were drowned in the noise. Some started to fall back.

From a nearby knoll, four American artillery guns began firing. With about twenty men, field commander Major Charles Plenderleath charged the position and captured the guns, turning them on their former owners. Confusion reigned.

"When it commenced to get daylight, we could see the enemy running in all directions," recalled Billy Green.

Both of the American generals were captured, one of them while he was attempting to rally troops he mistakenly identified as American. General Vincent fell from his horse and got lost in the bushes. He was discovered, horseless and hatless, that morning.

The battle lasted barely forty minutes. When it was over a native observer noted that corpses were strewn over the landscape like freshly caught salmon. Nearly one-third of the attacking British force were killed, wounded or missing.

American losses represented less than one-tenth of their force. However costly the victory was, it was enough to turn the Americans back, demoralized, leaderless, unaware of the diminished state of their adversaries.

On the battlefield, Billy Green and several Stoney Creek youths collected the bodies on an ox-drawn stoneboat and buried them.

Sixty-two years later, a grateful nation honoured Billy Green with a twenty-dollar gratuity. The following year, he died at the age of eighty-three.

Like his female counterpart, Laura Secord, Billy Green's bravery was barely acknowledged during his lifetime.

Ironically, following the war that defined the Canadian sense of uniquely un-American nationhood, Billy was often identified as "the Paul Revere of Canada."

SINK OR SWIM

Vancouver, 1886 — At Alexandra Park in the West End of Vancouver there is a marble fountain depicting three children splashing in the water beneath the face of a man. The inscription it bears reads: "Little Children loved Him."

Created by Italian-Canadian sculptor Charles Marega, the fountain is dedicated to legendary lifeguard, Seraphim "Joe" Fortes, who spent most of his life patrolling the beach of English Bay and teaching youngsters how to swim. In the process, he is credited with saving at least twenty-nine lives and spreading goodwill wherever he went.

Seraphim Fortes is believed to have grown up in the Caribbean on the island of Barbados. When he was a teenager he took to the seas and sailed to Liverpool, England where he worked as a bath attendant and swimming instructor for half a dozen years. Swimming was one thing that he excelled at and he received a medal from the daughter of the Lord Mayor of London for winning a race across the Mersey River.

In 1884, he boarded the vessel *Robert Kerr* and began a journey which was supposed to end at Victoria on Vancouver Island. Instead, the rag-tag ship lost its main mast and was towed into Vancouver's Burrard Inlet. By this time, Fortes was seldom known as "Seraphim," that celestial first name having been reduced to "Joe" by his shipmates during the voyage. As "Joe," the strapping, stout black man took a variety of jobs in the rough and tumble landscape of "Gastown," which had been populated and carved by colourful characters with names like Hog Ned, Dumps Baker, Hans the Boatman and the voluble Gassy Jack Deighton.

Although he was in his mid-thirties when he arrived in the area that is now known as Granville, Joe is noted to have been its first shoeshine "boy." He also worked as a bouncer at the Sunnyside Hotel, before moving on to the Bodega Saloon where he served as a teetotalling bartender who discouraged heavy product abuse. ·

On June 13, 1886, Fortes and all of Vancouver witnessed the conflagration of their community. It was a Sunday, but CPR crews who had been clearing massive tracts of timber for a new railway terminus were busy burning stumps and debris. By this time, the entire coast had been subjected to what has been termed *silvi-slaughter*. Douglas fir trees that measured as much as four metres (thirteen feet) at the base were felled by axemen, creating a domino-effect that crushed younger trees and left storey-high jumbles of trunks and limbs cluttering the landscape.

The pall of smoke was a constant as the CPR burned the slash. It had been a dry spring and that combined with a freakish blast of wind from the west allowed the fire between Hamilton and Granville Streets to grow so far out of control that comparisons were made to the volcano at Pompeii.

In less than an hour, a thousand wooden buildings were incinerated. Newspaper accounts said that wooden sidewalks burned faster than pedestrians could run. Roofs blew off buildings and flaming wood pelted down on citizens who tried to find safety in the water.

In the midst of it all, "Big Joe" was spotted helping the largely volunteer force of firefighters. Ironically, the ship that brought him to B.C., the abandoned *Robert Kerr*, had been blown from its anchorage off Deadman's Island to a reachable position near the beach. Several hundred people swam, rowed or paddled on logs to its safety. The heat was ferocious. Within minutes of the start of the fire the bell at St. James Church was ringing a warning. By the fire's end, the church was gone. Today, its melted bell is displayed at the Vancouver Museum.

In the only way he knew, protecting his fellow citizens from harm became Joe Fortes' mission as

Vancouver struggled to recover from the devastation. His massive smile and stature made him a popular figure on English Bay, where he swam every morning throughout the year, consuming a cup of salt water daily and calling it his "medicine." Three generations of Vancouverites credit him with teaching them how to swim.

"Jump! I tell you jump! If you don't jump off that raft, I'll throw you in," were the words that stuck in novelist Ethel Wilson's memory of Joe. And she jumped as did countless children at Joe's command.

"He taught nearly all the boys and girls to swim," wrote Wilson. "Joe was a heroic figure."

At the turn of the century, Fortes was made Vancouver's first official lifeguard and in 1904 he was made a Special Constable of the Auxiliary Police Force.

He lived in a tidy cottage by the beach, where he maintained the gender dividing-line between male and female bathers, and where he castigated litter-bugs. The lives he is officially credited with saving are said to be far fewer than those who would wish they could have been acknowledged. Storm waves could not keep him from a capsized boater.

When the city decided to demolish a row of squatter's cottages from the beach in the name of development, Joe's humble abode was moved to a place closer to the bandstand in the park where it was hung with a prestigious gift of the city in 1910 — an "illuminated address."

Sixty-year-old Joe Fortes died of pneumonia in February, 1922. At his packed funeral, the organ played "Old Black Joe" with all respect and the hearse towed his familiar rowboat which was filled with flowers.

Along with the fountain in his memory, there is a library named after Joe Fortes. And, of course, should you get hungry in Vancouver, you may want to try a bowl of the Westcoast Geoduck Clam Chowder "Manhattan Style," available at the restaurant that bears his Seraphim-less namesake.

WHITE LAMA

Chatham, Ontario to Tibet, 1895 — Bounded by the Yangtze River and three sets of mountains, the Himalayas, the Karakoram and the Kunlun, Tibet has been called "the Roof of the World." The spiritual homeland of the Dalai Lama was an exotic half a world away from the rural southwestern Ontario town of Chatham where Susanna Carson was born in 1868. But she would go there — twice — as a medical missionary.

Active in the Methodist church throughout childhood, the young woman who was known all her life as "Susie" had decided by the age of fourteen that she wanted to become a doctor. In fact, Susie was barely eleven when her progressive father, who was a principal and school inspector, began making inquiries about a Canadian medical course for women doctors.

At the age of twenty, Dr. Carson graduated from the second class of female students at Women's

Medical College in Toronto. With her sister, Jessie, another graduate of Women's Medical, she practised in Strathroy, Ontario until her marriage six year later to a Dutchman named Petrus Rijnhart.

Petrus had already travelled to China as part of a non-denominational mission, but he was turfed when his credentials were scrutinized and found lacking. In Toronto, he learned English by working at a factory and soon found supporters to back his idea of a mission to Tibet (Xizang province in the People's Republic of China).

Responding to what she viewed as a calling "to do pioneer work," Susie joined him on the odyssey across the ocean and across China, armed with everything from dental and surgical implements to copies of the scripture in Tibetan and a bicycle.

The Rijnharts settled in Lusar, a border town in Outer Tibet that was the trading centre for the lamasery of Kumbum, home to more than 4,000 lamas who followed the teachings of Buddha. Although foreign missionaries were generally regarded with suspicion, the Rijnharts were allowed to build a house and establish a medical clinic. A young lama taught them the language and they adapted to local customs, including drinking tea mixed with rancid butter and salt which they found less than savory.

Their evangelic efforts were deliberately subtle. Although the Rijnharts' mission was to convert Tibetans to their vision of Christianity, they recognized

Buddhism as a religion worthy of respect. "In every religious service, however absurd or degraded from the Christian point of view," Susie noted, "there is some feeble acknowledgement and groping after the one great God."

By decorating the walls of the surgery with provocative biblical illustrations, such as the story of Lazarus being risen from the dead, the Rijnharts were able to engage Tibetans in discussion. Their reputation as healers and the tactful way in which they introduced their religion without imposing it or attacking alternative forms of worship earned them the interest of curious Tibetans and a powerful friendship.

The kanpo (abbott) of the lamasery, Mina Fuyeh, invited Susie and Petrus to attend his ailing treasurer at his residence, an unheard-of privilege for a foreigner. Mina Fuyeh, a lively twenty-seven year old, was the highest dignitary in northeastern Tibet and ranked as a "living Buddha." He was interested in knowing everything about the Rijnharts' religion and studied the scriptures closely, finding many Christian precepts to be compatible with Buddhism. Naively, the Rijnharts held hope that Mina Fuyeh would convert, but their "firm friend" was not about to abdicate a position that had taken him many reincarnations to achieve.

When a Muslim rebellion threw the countryside into turmoil, Mina Fuyeh offered the Rijnharts sanctuary in the lamasery. From safety, they watched as thousands of lamas wearing red and yellow robes and silk turbans marched off to join Chinese troops in putting down the revolt. While the Rijnharts treated a diphtheria outbreak in the refugee-crowded monastery, villages were destroyed in brutal fighting that saw 100,000 killed. The "white lamas," as the Rijnharts were known, ended up going to the battlefields to treat the wounded.

The army surgeon and her public health officer endeared themselves to the Tibetan people, treating thousands of patients and never asking for payment. But Susie and Petrus never lost sight of the purpose that brought them to Tibet. On Wednesdays and Sundays they ran a Bible school. It was a popular gathering place for women and children, who sang the hymns they were taught to the accompaniment of Susie's violin and Petrus's concertina. Still, there were no converts.

Life in Lusar was good, but since the Rijnharts considered their mandate to be spreading the gospel, they accepted an invitation to take their work to Tankar, a trading town in Inner Tibet.

When Petrus was called away to Peking (Beijing) for several months, Susie felt comfortable and secure enough to stay alone in Tankar. In a country where foreigners sometimes disappeared or were murdered, this unusual circumstance surprised visiting Swedish explorer, Sven Hedrin. He might have been even more "astonished" at meeting the "bareheaded young lady wearing spectacles and dressed after the Chinese manner," if he had known that she was also pregnant. Charles Carson Rijnhart was born in July of 1897.

Restless and relentless, the Rijnharts conducted a number of itinerant missions, distributing gospels throughout the countryside. But they knew that the ultimate prize would be to enter the "Sealed Land," and carry the word of their God to Lhasa, the site of the most sacred of all Buddhist monasteries.

"The Lord had opened many doors for us in China, and we were confident He would open others," Susie wrote in her narrative memoir *With the Tibetans in Tent and Temple*. With their ten-month-old son and dog, Topsy, they set off with three guides to lead them through the mountains, a dozen pack horses carrying food for a year, and 500 copies of the New Testament.

After travelling for two hellish months through bogs, hail, torrential rains and snow with the constant threat of wild animals and thieves, they were about a week's journey away from their goal. It was late August when Susie wrote that "the darkest day in our lives arose bright and full of promise." By the end of it, their ailing baby was dead, despite all of Susie's efforts. The Rijnharts buried their "darling" with a bouquet of wild asters and blue poppies in their emptied drug box and covered it with a boulder.

At this point they had already lost five of their pack horses to thieves and their guides had deserted them. A government patrol tried to stop them, but they pressed on stealthily until they were finally turned back.

Reprovisioned with guides and horses, the Rijnharts were on their way to China when they were attacked by robbers who killed all but one of their horses and scared off their guides. Travelling through deep snow they came across a tented camp across a river.

On September 26, 1898, eleven days after the couple's fourth anniversary, Petrus left Susie alone with a revolver for protection. His plan was to swim across the river and enlist help. Susie never saw him again. Revolver in hand, she waited for three days, searching the river bank with her telescope.

It took Susie two months to reach a branch of the China Inland Mission at Tachienlu (Kangdon) in Szechuan province. Convinced that her husband had been murdered, she spent six months trying to find the culprits, to no avail.

Her health was failing and, at thirty-two, her hair was completely white when she returned to Chatham in 1900. She wrote her book and embarked on a lecture tour, but two years later she returned to Tibet. In 1905, she married a Scottish missionary, James Moyes, who had been the first white man to speak to her following Petrus's disappearance.

In 1907, Susie and James returned to Chatham. The following year, Susie died two months after giving birth to a daughter. Her sister was her attending physician. The mission she had founded in Tibet was closed, having recorded seven converts.

"If ever the gospel were proclaimed in Lhasa," Susie wrote, "someone would have to be the first to undertake the journey, to meet the difficulties, to preach the first sermon and perhaps never return to tell the tale — who knew?"

THE GREAT STORK DERBY

Toronto, 1926 to 1936 — No one has ever been able to explain exactly just what possessed Charlie Millar when he was drawing up his last will and testament. The prominent Toronto lawyer and sportsman was considered to be a "respectable stuffed shirt," shy, irascible and thrifty. But when he died at seventy-three, he sparked a breeding frenzy in Toronto the like of which had never been seen.

Provisions in the will set forth rules for a fecundity contest that would award the bulk of the bachelor Millar's considerable estate to the Toronto woman who produced the most children "under the Vital Statistics Act" between the date of his death on Halloween Day, 1926, and the marking of that event's tenth anniversary.

The contest became known as the "Great Stork Derby." When it ended, four women who fielded families the size of baseball teams were declared the winners. Each received $165,000.

Mothers who gave birth to only eight children were out of luck. One poor woman, Mae Clark, was also a loser even though she gave birth to ten children. Five of the Clark children were sired by Mae's legal husband, but five others were of questionable paternity. A righteous court ruled the illegitimate children out of the running, but the derby winners compensated Mrs. Clark with a gift of $12,500 to stave off further legal wrangles. All of the winners were of modest means. One family had been on welfare and they promptly returned the $1,800 that they had collected from the City.

In the preamble to his will, Charles Vance Millar stated that he intended its contents to be "uncommon and capricious."

He left nothing to his relatives, and little to his faithful employees.

"If I left them money they would be glad when I died," Millar once told a friend. "I don't want anybody to look forward to my death."

In death, however, Millar loomed much larger than in life. A farm boy from Aylmer, Ontario, he became a prize-winning student. After passing the bar, he started his career as a three-dollar-a-week lawyer living in Toronto's Queen's Hotel, where the manager gave him credit. Gradually, he built a booming business in corporate law and bought a dozen houses as rental properties. He owned a houseboat with the Chief Justice of the Ontario Supreme Court and once had two racehorses place first and second in the 1915 King's Plate.

When he died Millar's estate was valued at only $104,000. However, over the decade of the derby it grew almost tenfold when his once paltry stock portfolio skyrocketed due to the success of the Windsor-Detroit Tunnel Co., in which he held 100,000 shares.

The few bequests that he made to individuals were almost as controversial as the Stork Derby. He left one share of a Catholic-owned brewery to every Protestant minister in Toronto.

Of the 303 clergymen who qualified, 99 applied for their share and at least three shares were turned over for charitable uses.

Only thirteen of Toronto's 114 Orange Lodges declined the same offer.

Clergymen in the Windsor area were offered one share each in the Kennilworth Race Track, which raised moral questions until it was discovered that the shares were worth less than a penny a piece.

Three lawyers who were known to dislike each other were given Millar's vacation home in Jamaica.

A devout horse-racing enthusiast and two adversaries of the betting sport — the head of the Methodist Church in Canada and a former Attorney-General of Ontario — were each offered a fifteen-hundred-dollar share in the Ontario Jockey Club provided they enrolled in the club. The two anti-gamblers joined the club for five minutes, sold their shares for a modest profit and donated the proceeds to the Poppy Fund.

A series of relatives challenged the will to no avail, but the longest running litigation was pursued by the Ontario government, which argued that it was "against public policy" and encouraged immorality.

Eleven years after Millar's death a judge finally ended the debate, stating: "I cannot find that reproduction of the human race is contrary to morals." The "Millar Will" stood as a last testament to its maker's legal skills.

Line for line, the "Great Stork Derby" received more newspaper coverage than Charles Lindbergh and the stock market crash. "The things I remember most are the smell of many children in bad houses; the unnatural talk about big money by tired women on relief; the resigned resentment of husbands whose procreative powers had suddenly become world news," one reporter told *Maclean's* magazine twenty-five years later.

In his own eccentric way, Charlie Millar may have been trying to make a statement of opposition to the government of Ontario's ban on birth control information. However, the end product caused much grief to many who could ill afford it.

A friend suggested that: "Charlie's hope was that, by turning the spotlight on unbridled breeding and making us a laughing stock before the world he could shame the government into legalizing birth control."

That ultimate distinction fell to a twenty-eight-year-old clerk from Ottawa who was arraigned on charges of distributing birth control information and contraceptive devices ten days before the Stork Derby ended.

Welsh-born Dorothea Palmer was arrested in the predominantly French-speaking, Roman Catholic suburb of Eastview. She had been offering requested advice about contraception on behalf of the Parent's Information Bureau, where she was employed as a part-time social worker by A.R. Kaufman, a Kitchener, Ontario rubber goods manufacturer. Kaufman hired the best defence counsel that money could buy.

The trial lasted a remarkable six months. Forty witnesses were called, including experts ranging from psychologists to relief workers, professors and birth control experts. The case hinged on the notion that although Section 207 of the Criminal Code stated that it was a crime to sell or advertise contraceptive drugs or devices, no person could be convicted if they could show that they were acting in the public good.

Dorothea Palmer was acquitted on March 17, 1937. Thirty-two years later, the Criminal Code of Canada was amended and the dissemination of birth control information and contraceptive devices were finally legal.

A BELLY LAUGH
OR YOUR MONEY BACK

Lillooet, British Columbia, 1934 — She called herself "Ye Ed" but to most everyone else, Margaret Murray, the editor of British Columbia's *Bridge River-Lillooet News* was known as "Ma." Cut from a cloth which was both delightful and maddening to her readers, Ma Murray was an original and as irrepressible as *Calgary Eye Opener* editor Bob Edwards. In fact, the two mavericks were acquainted. In 1913, when Margaret Lally married her boss, editor George Murray, Bob Edwards sent champagne to their wedding table.

"Guarantees a chuckle every week and a belly laugh once a month or your money back," proclaimed Ma's masthead. The circulation of the community newspaper might have peaked at 2,000 but "every bloody one of 'em paid for" was proclaimed with blunt pride.

Irreverent, sometimes even shocking, Ma Murray spiced her editorials with words like "craporini," "damshur" and "snaffoo." She freely admitted that she was not a writer, rather she "told things." At the beginning of the year, readers who insisted on proper grammar were rewarded with two inches of punctuation marks to position as they saw fit.

A child of Irish immigrant parents, Margaret was raised on a farm in Windy Ridge, Kansas. Her childhood education stopped at Grade Three, but she washed dishes to pay tuition fees to attend secretarial school and graduated with honours.

While working at a saddlery company in Kansas City, Margaret started sending notes along with the invoices to Alberta cowboys, and was rewarded with return correspondence that included pictures of broad-shouldered Westerners, invitations and even marriage proposals. In 1912, her curiosity got the better of her and she headed for Calgary "to catch a cowboy." Her money ran out in Vancouver and she decided to stay.

She started out in the newspaper business selling subscriptions to *B.C. Federation*, a labour publication. This led to a bookkeeping job at a south Vancouver weekly called the *Chinook*, where she was soon writing community news.

"My boss is a nice young man, a little vague and annoying but real handsome," Margaret said in a letter home. Less than a year later, she married *Chinook* editor George Murray.

Two children and a series of newspapers followed, with poverty a constant companion. Margaret and the children homesteaded in a small tar-paper cottage on Burrard Inlet until George got a steady job as the managing editor of the *Vancouver Morning Sun*. Back in Vancouver, Margaret started *Country Life in B.C.* magazine, an enterprise that involved her in the activities of Women's Institutes and saw her reporting on everything from beekeeping to rug hooking.

Margaret claimed the Depression hit the Murray family a full year before the stock market crashed in 1929. George's salary was halved, the children were placed in boarding school and Margaret tried selling her homemade handicrafts. "Times were very hard," she recalled later. "My tongue was stickin' out a foot for a taste of a strip of bacon." But the characteristic Murray optimism never failed.

George felt strongly about the need for development in B.C. and improved transportation corridors to the north. With Margaret's help and a $200 campaign budget, he was elected to the provincial legislature in 1933 as the Liberal member for Lillooet, a small interior community that was noted as Mile One during the Caribou gold rush.

"Well hells bells, we're here aren't we, so we may as well start a newspaper,'" announced Margaret.

According to her daughter, Georgina, the family settled in "a house that looked ready to slip into the Fraser River before dinnertime." The salt-box, frame house ringed with porches was the heart of the newspaper Margaret founded in 1934 to help supplement George's meagre salary as an MLA.

An upstairs bedroom served as the editorial office. A hole was cut in the floor so that copy could be lowered to the waiting press, a Klondike gold rush artifact that shook the whole building when it rolled. Margaret sold advertising and subscriptions, sometimes accepting chickens in lieu of cash. At fifty-three, she was running her own newspaper and Margaret Murray felt she had come into her own.

Other people may have thought that "Ye Ed" came a bit too close to coming into their own. The *Bridge River-Lillooet News* was cited in seven divorce actions after publishing a local hotel's guest registry. And Margaret's expansive editorial language raised legal hassles. The *News* paid legal costs when a retraction on behalf of an individual who was described as a "crooked horse trader" and a "gypsy," was not forthcoming.

Margaret found news everywhere she looked. She covered everything from gold strikes to prostitution and pulled no punches.

"I'm the editor of the dinkiest paper in British Columbia," she once told a television interviewer. "The place I live in is so isolated you gotta scrape the bottom of the barrel. My God, there isn't a week I don't have slivers in my fingers scrapin' up the news."

A Toronto writer provided the moniker "Ma" and even though Margaret disliked it at first, her weekly column "My Week, A Digest of the More Homely Things in Our Everyday Life," was soon signed "Ma Murray."

The Murray publishing empire expanded to include at least two more newspapers, which were soon under the management of their children. The Second World War brought changes to British Columbia. In 1942, Lillooet became an internment centre for more than 3,000 Japanese Canadians. At the same time, George Murray's dream of a highway to Alaska was being realized as American dollars poured into the construction of a defence road following the Japanese occupation of the Aleutian Islands. The Murrays decided to move where the action was, settling in Fort St. John, north of Dawson City in the Peace River Valley where the first issue of the *Alaska Highway News* appeared in 1944.

Coincidentally, during that period George was defeated after serving eight years in the legislature, and prosperity in Fort St. John declined when American troops stationed along the new highway pulled out.

"What kind of heebie jeebies has hit this town anyway?" Ma wrote of the slump. "Checks in this town are bouncing like popcorn and pockets are empty."

Although Margaret had briefly flirted with developing her own political career as a Social Credit candidate, George remained staunchly Liberal. In 1949, he was elected as the federal member in the Cariboo riding. Ma, however, did not last long in Ottawa. Although her son Dan had agreed to run the newspaper, apparently the two could not see eye-to-eye on editorial or subscription policy. When she returned for a visit, he had gone and she stayed to run the paper.

In 1958, the Murrays decided to retire in Vancouver and their children took over the *Alaksa Highway News*. Three months later, seventy-one year-old Ma Murrary informed her daughter that she felt "no sap flowing inside." The couple returned to Lillooet and bought back the old newspaper. A few years later, George died, but "Ye Ed" continued to produce her newspaper well into her eighties, including the popular column "Chat Out of the Old Bag." She never lost the "dinging away" edge that both delighted and infuriated her readers.

"Governments are like underwear. They start smelling pretty bad if you don't change them once in a while," Ma told the Toronto *Star* at the 1981 premiere of Eric Nichol's play *Ma! A Celebration of Margaret Murray*. The following year Margaret Murray was buried beside her husband in Fort St. John. She was ninety-five.

A MALTESE FALCON

Verdun, Quebec to Malta, 1942 — Heroes are heroes by any name. However, "Screwball" wasn't quite the public relations moniker the government had in mind when it sent Canadian flying ace, George Beurling, on a public speaking tour to raise money for the war effort. So, "Screwball" became "Buzz," but that made little impression on the grounded pilot. He was a flyer, an airborne killer and a ruthless lone wolf, not a fund-raiser, and certainly not a groundling.

"If I were ever asked to do that again, I'd tell them to go to hell or else ask for a commission on the bonds I sold," Beurling told a reporter. The war bond effort was better off without him. George Beurling's mission was fighting in the terrifying skies of World War II.

Born in 1921 in Verdun, Quebec, George was fascinated with airplanes from childhood. He built model airplanes with his father, becoming so proficient that he was able to sell his handiwork and use the money for flying lessons. He analyzed World War I aerial battles and tactics the way other children studied National Hockey League trades and statistics. According to his father, George "ate, drank and slept airplanes and air fighting."

By the time he was fourteen, George was taking weekly flying lessons. At seventeen, he left his religious family behind and got a job in Ontario as a bush pilot hauling freight and accumulating enough flying hours to earn his pilot's licence. Then he rode the rails to Vancouver where he tried to enlist in the Chinese air force, which was fighting the Japanese invasion of Manchuria.

Along the way, he sought out WW I ace Ernst Udet, whose Allied kills placed him second only to the infamous "Red Baron" Manfred Von Richtofen. Udet was performing in barnstorming events, but George Beurling persuaded him (with cash) to teach him the dogfighting tactics of aerial warfare.

George never did get to China. Instead, he turned to the Royal Canadian Air Force. Despite the fact that Beurling had won a flying aerobics competition in Edmonton and beaten two RCAF pilots, he was rejected. Recruiters suggested that he would be better off completing his last year of high school.

The Finnish air force would have taken Beurling, but he was just eighteen and his parents would not give their permission. So George took a different tact. He headed for Glasgow as a deckhand on a munitions ship.

On landing, Beurling presented himself to Britain's Royal Air Force, but he was missing vital papers, including his birth certificate. He sailed back to Canada on the Valparaiso, dodging German U-boats and surviving a torpedo attack. After crossing the ocean three times, Beurling was finally accepted in the RAF.

During training, he impressed his instructors so much that he was asked to accept a commission and stay on as a teacher. Beurling declined. He wanted action.

In formation, he was a "Tail-End-Charlie," flying his Spitfire aircraft behind and slightly above four other fighters. It was the most hazardous position.

To put it lightly, from the outset Sergeant Beurling had difficulty accepting authority figures. If he saw an opportunity in the air he would take it, even if that meant disobeying orders, and especially if it meant taking a chance to attack the enemy or alert his fellow-flyers to danger. Further, when he felt orders lacked intellectual or practical merit, he expressed his opinion. One of his biographers has suggested that he volunteered for service at the height of the siege of Malta because he was "disgusted with the crass stupidity of his commanding officers."

Beurling arrived in Malta in the middle of an air raid. The Germans and Italians were maintaining a constant assault on the critically located Island. Laddie Lucas was Beurling's new commanding officer in the all-Canadian RAF Spitfire Squadron and he recognized

Beurling's rebellious ego, but he also saw in that some deeper sense of inferiority and a need for mutual trust.

"I judged that what Beurling needed was not to be smacked down but to be encouraged," Lucas said later. "He never let me down."

In his first month, Beurling shot down five, possibly six, enemy aircraft. He used the dogfighting tricks Udet had taught him — making tight circles, firing from what seemed to be impossible angles. His expertise lay in the "deflection shot." With deadly precision he could calculate distance, speed and angles in the air, determining in an instant when and where the line of fire between his guns and the enemy would "harmonize."

"He used to report sighting of aircraft many seconds before others saw them," said one of his fellow pilots. "And he knew whether he hit them in the front, centre or rear of their airplane and he usually used minimum ammunition."

Like World War I ace Billy Bishop, Beurling was a master of surprise and sneak attacks. He would watch an enemy squadron, assess the talents of the pilots he was confronting and then try to take out the best first.

"There is no room for softheartedness," he told *Maclean's* magazine writer Webb Waldron. "The enemy is trying to get you, it is up to you to get him first — hard and plenty."

Occasionally, Beurling would line his plane up in a head-on confrontation, shooting to kill the oncoming pilot, and then peeling away to attack any chasers. Other pilots dubbed him "Screwball," but Laddie Lucas said there wasn't anything wild about the way Beurling conducted himself in the air, he was just accurate in what he did.

Citations began accumulating. Despite his protests, Beurling was ordered to accept an officer's commission. Ultimately he would receive the Distinguished Service Order, the Distinguished Flying Medal with a bar for bravery and the Distinguished Flying Cross.

The war in the air over Malta that summer was brutal. Pilots were shot as they hung in their parachutes. As the temperature rose, so did tempers. The Germans and Italians attempted to cut supplies to the Island and food was scarce. Pilots lived in caves or sat in their aircraft waiting for reports of a raid, conserving gasoline until a last-minute scramble was called.

Like many other exhausted pilots, Beurling lost a lot of weight and was bed-ridden for a week with malnutrition and a disease they called "the Dog."

In October, 1942, half of Beurling's squad was shot down. Raids were constant. He was flying a shift every day. On his last flight over Malta, Beurling led a squadron of eight Spitfires against eight enemy bombers and fifty fighters.

He shot down one bomber, but as it fell the rear gunner returned fire hitting Beurling's fingers and forearm. Beurling then turned his sights on a German fighter in front of him. While wounding it, he came under fire, suffering damage to the Spitfire's tail and wings.

"Screwball" went into a power dive heading straight for the sea before pulling up under the German formation and shooting down another fighter. This attracted the attention of the enemy. Beurling's controls where shot out and shrapnel ripped into one of his feet. The scene he described was the nightmare of every pilot.

"My plane was on fire, flames coming out toward me. I tried to climb out of the cockpit, but centrifugal force pressed me into my seat. I fought to get out and at the last minute I did manage to jump. Another split second and it would have been too late."

Beurling's parachute opened less than 1,000 feet above the water. When he was plucked out of the blood-stained Mediterranean, his only concern was for the Bible he always flew with, one his mother had given him.

In four months, he had shot down seventeen enemy planes over Malta. After a period of hospital-ization, Beurling was shipped back to Britain and then sent to Canada on the war bond–selling mission — as "Buzz" not "Screwball."

Afterwards, the RAF wanted him as a gunnery instructor in England, but Beurling wanted to be back in the air. He transferred to the Royal Canadian Air Force in northern France. The final confirmed tally of

Beurling's victories is thirty-one, although others may have fallen, wounded and out of sight.

Beurling's troubles with authority continued in France. After facing discipline for flying too low over his own airfield, Beurling resigned with an honourable discharge.

The United States Air Force rejected him. Ottawa would not permit him to join the Chinese against Mao Tse-tung. Commercial airlines turned him down, as well. Without an airplane or an enemy, Beurling's life fell apart. At one point, he was reduced to begging in the streets of Montreal.

Postwar tension in the Middle East presented an opportunity. Beurling was twenty-seven when he hired on as a fighter with the newly formed Israeli Air Force in 1948.

What happened next remains a mystery. Beurling arrived in Rome en route to Tel Aviv. Some say that he died alone, crashing almost inexplicably on a familiarization flight. Others say he was piloting a plane carrying former Luftwaffe pilots who were also bound for Israel. In that account, an engine died after takeoff and Beurling heroically steered the plane away from a populated area before the plane stalled and crashed killing all aboard. More sinister conjecture suggests the British Foreign Service and Secret Service planted a bomb in the plane to thwart the Israelis.

When he was inducted into Canada's Aviation Hall of Fame in 1973, the citation honouring George

Frederick Beurling read: "The brilliance of air fighting tactics, performed in a self-imposed area of loneliness with a structured military command, recall earlier wartime standards of heroic personal determination and have been of outstanding benefit to Canadian aviation."

He was the falcon of Malta.

"DON'T LET
THE CRIPPLED KIDS DOWN"

Lake Ontario, 1954 — Before she started her marathon swim across Lake Ontario, Marilyn Bell said she thought she would scream if she felt an eel on her body. But when it happened — when a pencil-long lamprey eel fixed its disc-shaped excuse for a mouth to the stomach of her black silk and nylon bathing suit, in the middle of the night, in the pitch blackness of Lake Ontario — Marilyn just hauled back and punched the sucker. Three more lampreys would assail her thighs, but the young woman calmly beat them off and kept on swimming.

There were other slippery creatures in the boats that surrounded her, but Marilyn never had to hit a newspaper reporter. They were too busy battling among themselves for her story. She was headline news; an unknown schoolgirl attempting to become the first swimmer to conquer Lake Ontario.

When she kissed her parents and dove off of a retaining wall in Youngstown, New York at 11:07 p.m. on September 8, 1954, Marilyn Bell was a sixteen-year-old Grade Twelve student at Toronto's Loretto College School. Just 155 centimetres (five feet one inch) and 54 kilograms (119 pounds), she was a finely tuned, blue-eyed pixie with a toothsome smile.

Her father, Syd, taught her to swim when she was four. By the age of ten, she was winning awards and medals. At thirteen she was teaching swimming lessons to children who had been crippled by polio and at fourteen she became a professional instructor.

Training under Gus Ryder, one of the top coaches in the country, she won numerous amateur races. As a teenaged professional, she was the first woman to complete the twenty-six-mile Atlantic City Marathon.

Still, veteran sports reporter Trent Frayne once noted: "Marilyn looked like somebody's baby-sitter."

The whole idea of the swim started with the Canadian National Exhibition, which hoped to attract crowds by featuring an American champion in a solo swim. They paid thirty-four-year-old, Californian Florence Chadwick $2,500 in advance, with a guarantee of $7,500 if she succeeded. The Toronto *Telegram* co-sponsored the promotion of the event. If there was a story in Chadwick's attempt, the *Tely* would have the inside edge.

However, marathon swimming was considered slightly past its prime. In 1927, seventeen-year-old

Torontonian George Young gained some margin of fame for swimming the Catalina Channel in California. The Catalina Kid's last successful marathon had gone virtually unnoticed in 1931.

When Marilyn Bell and St. Thomas, Ontario's Winnie Roach Leusler, twenty-eight, announced their plans to challenge Chadwick for free, the *Tely* wasn't much interested in the story, even though Winnie was the only Canadian who had swum the English Channel.

Gus Ryder offered both the *Telegram* and its arch rival, the Toronto *Star*, the opportunity to sponsor his swimmer and help underwrite costs including the $700 per day boat rental. The *Star* seized the opportunity. Marilyn also had the moral support of *Star* sports reporter Alexandrine Gibb, founder of the Women's Amateur Athletic Federation of Canada.

The race would begin when Florence Chadwick entered the water. Marilyn had made it known that her only fears were eels and swimming in the dark. For two days, weather delayed the start. When it finally cleared, Chadwick announced that she would start swimming shortly before midnight.

Marilyn Bell had not slept all day. Now she was facing fifty kilometres (thirty-two miles) of unlit, open water. She was only seven minutes behind Chadwick when she started, sprinting after Chadwick with her white bathing cap bobbing in the searchlights. Underneath it, tucked in her short blond hair, Marilyn had a four-leaf clover.

Five hours later, after stroking against the wind and confronting waves twice her height, a gaunt Marilyn treaded water while coach Ryder passed her a cup of corn syrup on a stick. She told him she was numb and cold, but he assured her that things would be better once the sun came up.

In the light of day, Marilyn looked rough; she was crying and her body ached. This time Coach Ryder passed her a cup of liniment to rub on her aching legs. The other swimmers were already out of the race, Flo overcome by nausea and Minnie pulled sobbing and cramp-riddled after two attempts.

At 10:30 a.m., after she had spent almost twelve hours in the water and gone more than twenty-four hours without sleep, Ryder pulled out a blackboard and wrote "FLO IS OUT" to offer Marilyn some encouragement. By noon, he turned to a more diabolical psychological ploy. The blackboard now read: "DON'T LET THE CRIPPLED KIDS DOWN."

Radio stations announced progress reports every half hour, while boatloads of reporters swarmed to get close enough for a photograph. People began flocking to the lakefront. Marilyn's classmates joined them, flowers in hand. By the time rush hour hit, the whole town knew the name "Marilyn Bell."

Having lost their American drawing card, CNE officials announced that the $7,500 Flo Chadwick had forfeited would now go to Marilyn if she finished.

Gus Ryder dutifully wrote the sum on his blackboard, but Marilyn could barely see it through her half-closed, bloodshot eyes.

Safety concerns grew amid a mounting flotilla of watercraft ranging from the tugboat *Ned Hanlan* to rowboats. The Toronto Harbour Commission sent lifeguards in dinghies to row alongside the wearying Marilyn. The waves had calmed but strong currents in the lake pushed her westward. Her stroke had slowed to fifty per minute.

Reporters in the Toronto *Star* boat ferried a fellow swimming instructor, Joan Cooke, out for moral support. Wearing a blouse and pedal-pushers, she swam to the coaching lifeboat and shivered out calls of encouragement to her friend.

Around five o'clock, Marilyn announced that her legs were totally numb and she had constant pain in her stomach. At Ryder's urging, Joan stripped down to her bra and panties, joining a dozing Marilyn in the lake, where she cajoled the exhausted teenager into following her pace for a few minutes.

As darkness fell, chill winds picked up. CNE officials became concerned that instead of landing at the Exhibition grounds where pink flares lit the sky, Marilyn seemed to be on a course to the west and Sunnyside Park. With just three kilometres (approximately two miles) to go, Syd Bell screamed at officials to "get out of here." He was ready to take his sobbing child out of the water, but Gus

Ryder shouted to Marilyn, asking her for just fifteen minutes more.

A huge headline in the *Tely* read "ONLY YARDS TO GO." Across Canada, radio audiences were glued to their sets. A crowd estimated at 250,000 whooped and roared, while the motley armada on the lake let off whistles and sirens. The only thing missing was a fledgling media called television. The local CBC station opted to cover a social event rather than the human interest story of the year.

Unbeknownst to Marilyn, the Harbour Commissioner had decreed that Marilyn's swim would be deemed successful if she reached the offshore breakwater. After almost twenty hours in the water, her left hand touched the concrete at 8:06 p.m. Fireworks filled the sky. Two lifeguards had a difficult time removing Marilyn from the water. She kept insisting she was "all right."

Marilyn didn't know that she had legitimately succeeded in her goal until she was in the back of an ambulance.

Right down to the wire, the *Telegram* and the *Star* vied for the story. *Tely* editor J.D. MacFarlane even went so far as to have a female reporter disguised as a nurse attempt to lure Bell into the *Telegram* ambulance and take her away. The attempted kidnapping was foiled when *Star* reporters discovered that the untended *Tely* ambulance had been left at curbside with the keys in the ignition. They moved it a few blocks, pocketing the keys and the distributor cap for good measure. That didn't stop the *Tely*'s intrepid "Nurse" Dorothy Horwath from trying to sneak aboard the *Star*'s official ambulance. She was ejected. However, the next day, the *Telegram* appeared to have scooped the *Star*. It ran a first-person story next to the signature "Marilyn Bell," which had been lifted from the inside cover of one of her school books.

Marilyn became an instant celebrity, receiving $50,000 in prize money, gifts and contracts. Despite concerns about her health, she was in fine shape after a few days' rest. The following year, she crossed the English Channel. In 1956, she swam the Juan de Fuca Strait, reaching Victoria, B.C. in eleven hours and thirty-five minutes on her second attempt.

"It's okay if you fail at something," she once said, "as long as you don't give up — as long as you say — 'Okay, I will try it again!'"

Since 1954, more than thirty Canadian swimmers have crossed Lake Ontario. Their names are etched on a monument at Niagara-on-the-Lake and the list continues to grow. After the tragic loss of an American swimmer in 1974, all races are carefully monitored for the safety of the athletes. Some swimmers, such as Kim Middleton and John Scott, have made the swim more than once. Vicki Keith holds the record at five, including one all-butterfly crossing and a remarkable two-way swim in 1987.

Twenty years after Marilyn Bell's epic effort, another sixteen year old became the second Canadian woman to make the swim. Mrs. Marilyn Bell-DiLascio, the "Queen of the Lake," was on hand to congratulate Cindy Nicholas on a record time of fifteen hours and ten minutes.

"It's your lake now," she said with the aplomb of a champion.